Make-Believe

A Children's Play in a Prologue and Three Acts

A. A. Milne

A Samuel French Acting Edition

SAMUELFRENCH-LONDON.CO.UK
SAMUELFRENCH.COM

Revised © 1925 by A. A. Milne
Copyright © 1925 by A. A. Milne
All Rights Reserved

MAKE-BELIEVE is fully protected under the copyright laws of the British Commonwealth, including Canada, the United States of America, and all other countries of the Copyright Union. All rights, including professional and amateur stage productions, recitation, lecturing, public reading, motion picture, radio broadcasting, television and the rights of translation into foreign languages are strictly reserved.

ISBN 978-0-573-05014-5

www.samuelfrench-london.co.uk

www.samuelfrench.com

FOR AMATEUR PRODUCTION ENQUIRIES

UNITED KINGDOM AND WORLD EXCLUDING NORTH AMERICA

plays@SamuelFrench-London.co.uk

020 7255 4302/01

Each title is subject to availability from Samuel French,
depending upon country of performance.

CAUTION: Professional and amateur producers are hereby warned that *MAKE-BELIEVE* is subject to a licensing fee. Publication of this play does not imply availability for performance. Both amateurs and professionals considering a production are strongly advised to apply to the appropriate agent before starting rehearsals, advertising, or booking a theatre. A licensing fee must be paid whether the title is presented for charity or gain and whether or not admission is charged.

The professional rights in this play are controlled by Curtis Brown Ltd, Haymarket House, 28-29 Haymarket, London SW1Y 4SP.

No one shall make any changes in this title for the purpose of production. No part of this book may be reproduced, stored in a retrieval system, or transmitted in any form, by any means, now known or yet to be invented, including mechanical, electronic, photocopying, recording, videotaping, or otherwise, without the prior written permission of the publisher. No one shall upload this title, or part of this title, to any social media websites.

The right of A. A. Milne to be identified as author of this work has been asserted by him in accordance with Section 77 of the Copyright, Designs and Patents Act 1988

THE CHARACTERS

THE PROLOGUE.

Rosemary.
James.

Nine Hubbard Children.

ACT 1.

The Princess.
The Woodcutter.
The King.
The Queen.

Two attendants.
The Red Prince.
The Blue Prince.
The Yellow Prince.

ACT 2.

The Curate.
Oliver.
Miss Pinniger.
Jill.
Aunt Jane.
The Doctor.
The Pirate Chief.

Eight Pirates and Dusky Maidens.
Tua-Heeta.
The Missionary.
The Cassowary.
The Cannibal.
The Steward.

ACT 3.

Mr. and Mrs. Hubbard.
Peter Ableways.
Jonas Humphrey.
Martha Porritt.
Jennifer.
Bill.
Liz.

A Policeman.
Father Christmas.
Two Ushers.
Robinson Crusoe.
Riding Hood.
Bluebeard.
Goldilocks.

Make-Believe was first produced at the Lyric Theatre, Hammersmith, on December 24, 1918. The chief parts were played by MARJORY HOLMAN, JEAN CADELL, ROSA LYND, BETTY CHESTER, ROY LENNOL, JOHN BARCLAY, KINSEY PEILE, STANLEY DREWITT, IVAN BERLYN, and HERBERT MARSHALL—several parts each.

MAKE-BELIEVE

PROLOGUE

The playroom of the HUBBARD FAMILY—*nine of them. Counting* MR. *and* MRS. HUBBARD, *we realize that there are eleven* HUBBARDS *in all, and you would think that one at least of the two people we see in the room would be a* HUBBARD *of sorts. But no. The tall, manly figure is* JAMES, *the* HUBBARDS' *butler, for the* HUBBARDS *are able to afford a butler now. How different from the time when Old Mother Hubbard—called " old " because she was at least twenty-two, and " mother " because she had a passion for children—could not even find a bone for her faithful terrier; but, of course, that was before* HENRY *went into work. Well, the tall figure is* JAMES, *the butler, and the little one is* ROSEMARY, *a friend of the* HUBBARD FAMILY. ROSEMARY *is going in for literature this afternoon, as it's raining, and* JAMES *is making her quite comfortable first with pens and ink and blotting-paper—always so important when one wants to write. He has even thought of a stick of violet sealing-wax; after that there can be no excuse.*

ROSEMARY (*sitting*). Thank you, James. If anyone calls I am not at home.

JAMES. Yes, Miss. I mean, no, Miss.

ROSEMARY. You may add that I am engaged in writing my auto—autobiography.

JAMES. No, Miss. I mean, yes, Miss.

ROSEMARY. It's what every one writes, isn't it, James?

JAMES. I believe so, Miss.

ROSEMARY. Thank you. (*He goes to the door.*) Oh, James?

JAMES. Yes, Miss?

ROSEMARY. What *is* an autobiography?

JAMES. Well, I couldn't rightly say, Miss—not to explain it properly.

ROSEMARY (*dismayed*). Oh, James! . . . I thought you knew everything.

JAMES. In the ordinary way, yes, Miss, but every now and then——

ROSEMARY. It's very upsetting.

JAMES. Yes, Miss. . . . How would it be to write a play instead? Very easy work, they tell me.

ROSEMARY (*nodding*). Yes, that's much better. I'll write a play. Thank you, James.

JAMES. Not at all, Miss.

(*He goes out.*)

(ROSEMARY *bites her pen, and thinks deeply. At last she holds up her hands as the inspiration comes.*)

ROSEMARY (*as she writes*). Make-Believe. M-a-k-e hyphen B-e-l—— (*She stops and frowns.*) Now which way *is* it ? (*She tries it on the blotting-paper.*) That looks wrong. (*She tries it again.*) So does that. Oh, dear ! (*She rings the bell* . . . JAMES *returns.*)

JAMES. Yes, Miss ?

ROSEMARY. James, I have decided to call my play Make-Believe.

JAMES. Yes, Miss.

ROSEMARY (*carelessly*). When you spell " believe," it *is* " i-e," isn't it ?

JAMES. Yes, Miss.

ROSEMARY. I thought at first it was " e-i."

JAMES. Now you mention it, I think it is, Miss.

ROSEMARY (*reproachfully*). Oh, James ! Aren't you certain ?

JAMES. M-a-k-e, make, B-e-l—— (*He stops and scratches his whiskers.*)

ROSEMARY. Yes. *I* got as far as that.

JAMES. B-e-l——

ROSEMARY. You see, James, it spoils the play if you have an accident to the very first word of it.

JAMES. Yes, Miss. B-e-l—— I've noticed sometimes that if one writes a word careless-like on the blotting-paper, and then looks at it with the head on one side, there's a sort of instinct comes over one, as makes one say (*with a shake of the head*) " Rotten." One can then write it the other way more hopeful.

ROSEMARY. I've tried that.

JAMES. Then might I suggest, Miss, that you give it another name altogether ? As it might be, " Susan's Saturday Night," all easy words to spell, or " Red Revenge," or——

ROSEMARY. No. I *must* call it Make-Believe, because it's all of the play I've thought of so far.

JAMES. Quite so, Miss. Then how would it be to spell it wrong on purpose ? It comes funnier that way sometimes.

ROSEMARY. Does it ?

JAMES. Yes, Miss. Makes 'em laugh.

ROSEMARY. Oh ! . . . Well, which *is* the wrong way ?

JAMES. Ah, there you've got me again, Miss.

ROSEMARY (*inspired*). I know what I'll do. I'll spell it " i-e " ; and if it's right, then I'm right, and if it's wrong, then I'm funny.

JAMES. Yes, Miss. That's the safest.

ROSEMARY. Thank you, James.
JAMES. Not at all, Miss.

(*He goes out.*)

ROSEMARY (*writing*). Make-Believe. A Christmas Entertainment—— (*She stops and thinks, and then shakes her head.*) No, play—a Christmas Play in three acts. Er—— (*She is stuck.*)

(*Enter* JAMES.)

JAMES. Beg pardon, Miss, but the Misses and Masters Hubbard are without, and crave admittance.
ROSEMARY. All nine of them?
JAMES. Without having counted them, Miss, I should say that the majority of them were present.
ROSEMARY. Did you say that I was not at home?
JAMES. Yes, Miss. They said that, this being their house, and you being a visitor, if you *had* been at home, then you wouldn't have been here. Humour on the part of Master Bertram, Miss.
ROSEMARY. It's very upsetting when you're writing a play.
JAMES. Yes, Miss. Perhaps they could help you with it. The more the merrier, as you might say.
ROSEMARY. What a good idea, James. Admit them.
JAMES. Yes, Miss. (*He opens the door and says very rapidly.*) The Misses Ada, Caroline, Elsie, Gwendoline, and Isabel Hubbard, The Masters Bertram, Dennis, Frank, and Harold Hubbard. (*They come in.*)
ROSEMARY. How do you do?
ADA. Rosemary, darling, what *are* you doing? (*at* ROSEMARY'S *shoulder*). Oh, I say, she's writing a play!

(*Uproar and turmoil, as they all rush at* ROSEMARY.)

THE BOYS. ⎧ Coo! I say, shove me into it. What's it about?
         ⎨ Bet it's awful rot.
THE GIRLS. ⎩ Oh, Rosemary! Am *I* in it? Do tell us about it.
           Is it for Christmas?
ROSEMARY (*in alarm*). James, could you——?
JAMES (*firmly*). Silence, all. (*Order is restored.*)
ROSEMARY. Thank you, James. . . . Yes, it's a play for Christmas, and it is called "Make-Believe," and that's all I'm certain about yet, except that we're all going to be in it.
ALL. Hurrah!
BERTRAM. Then I vote we have a desert island——
DENNIS. And pirates——
FRANK. And cannibals——
HAROLD (*gloatingly*). Cannibals eating people—Oo!
CAROLINE (*shocked*). Harold! How would *you* like to be eaten by a cannibal?
DENNIS. Oh, chuck it! How would *you* like to be a cannibal

and have nobody to eat ? (CAROLINE *is silent, never having thought of this before.*)

ADA. Let it be a fairy-story, Rosemary, darling. It's so much prettier.

ELSIE. With a lovely princess——

GWENDOLINE. And a humble woodcutter who marries her——

ISABEL (*her only contribution*). P'itty P'incess.

BERTRAM. Princesses are rot.

ELSIE (*with spirit*). So are pirates ! (*Deadlock.*)

CAROLINE. *I* should like something about Father Christmas, and snow, and waits, and a lovely ball, and everybody getting nice presents and things.

DENNIS (*selfishly, I'm afraid*). Bags I all the presents.

(*Of course, the others aren't going to have that. They all say so together.*)

ROSEMARY (*above the turmoil and banging the table*). James, I *must* have silence.

JAMES. Silence, all !

ROSEMARY. Thank you. . . . You will be interested to hear that I have decided to have a Fairy Story *and* a Desert Island *and* a Father Christmas.

ALL. Good ! (*Or words to that effect.*)

ROSEMARY (*biting her pen*). I shall begin with the Fairy story. (*There is an anxious silence. None of them has ever seen anybody writing a play before. How does one do it ? Alas,* ROSEMARY *herself doesn't know. She appeals to* JAMES.) James, how do you begin a play ? I mean when you've *got* the title.

JAMES (*a man of genius*). Well, Miss Rosemary, seeing that it's to be called " Make-Believe," why not make-believe as it's written already ?

ALL. Ha ! Ha !

ROSEMARY. What a good idea, James !

JAMES. All that is necessary is for the company to think very hard of what they want, and—there we are ! Saves all the bother of writing and spelling and what not.

ROSEMARY. Now then, let's all think together. Are you all ready ?

CAROLINE. Stop a minute ! We must have music in our play.

ROSEMARY. Of course. Mr. . . . (*addressing conductor*), do your best.

Song.

LOVE AND LAUGHTER.

(*Song :* QUEEN OF MELODY.)

QUEEN. Children dear, whose little eyes
First were closed to lullabies,
It is yours to wander free
In the land of Melody.

MAKE-BELIEVE.

Songs of joyance and of pleasure,
Lilting theme and tripping measure,
Happy days of love and gladness,
But to-night, no songs of sadness.

    Chorus : Let there be song !

QUEEN. A song of love and laughter,
And of "happy ever after."
Let there be song !
Of lullaby, of playtime,
Of lovers in the May time,
In the land where all goes right
    and nothing wrong.

There shall be songs of pirate gold,
Of dusky maids and lovers bold,
Of tropic isles in flaming June,
And carols 'neath a frosty moon,
Of Christmas revels and the toys,
Beloved of little girls and boys.
All these and more I give to you
Because you know that I am true.

    Chorus : Let there be song !

Black out : followed by Act I.)

ACT I

THE PRINCESS AND THE WOODCUTTER

THE WOODCUTTER'S SONG

(WOODCUTTER.)

A humble woodman I,
A plain hard-working peasant,
A simple soul, who on the whole
Finds life extremely pleasant.
I envy none to-day
His lofty rank or station,
Enough for me to have a free
And healthy occupation.

Refrain : Singing and swinging my axe
On the monarch uprearing,
Stroke upon stroke, till the oak
Crashes down in the clearing.
So shall I vanquish, perchance,
Both the haughty and splendid,
Love shall have brought them to naught
When the tale shall be ended.

In realms of faery lore
I need no guide or tutor,
And there I learn princesses yearn
To wed the humble suitor.
The truly noble mind
All outward show despises;
It is not rank or wealth or swank
That takes the highest prizes !

Refrain (As before).

The WOODCUTTER *is discovered singing at his work, in a glade of the forest outside his hut. He is tall and strong, and brave and handsome; all that a woodcutter ought to be. Now it happened that the* PRINCESS *was passing, and as soon as his song is finished, sure enough, on she comes.*

PRINCESS. Good morning, Woodcutter.
WOODCUTTER. Good morning. (*But he goes on with his work.*)
PRINCESS (*after a pause*). Good morning, Woodcutter.
WOODCUTTER. Good morning.
PRINCESS. Don't you ever say anything except good morning ?
WOODCUTTER. Sometimes I say good-bye.
PRINCESS. You *are* a cross woodcutter to-day.

WOODCUTTER. I have work to do.

PRINCESS. You are still cutting wood ? Don't you ever do anything else ?

WOODCUTTER. Well, you are still a Princess ; don't *you* ever do anything else ?

PRINCESS (*reproachfully*). Now, that's not fair, Woodcutter. You can't say I was a Princess yesterday, when I came and helped you stack your wood. Or the day before, when I tied up your hand where you had cut it. Or the day before that, when we had our meal together on the grass. Was I a Princess then ?

WOODCUTTER. Somehow I think you were. Somehow I think you were saying to yourself, " Isn't it sweet of a Princess to treat a mere woodcutter like this ? "

PRINCESS. I think you're perfectly horrid. I've a good mind never to speak to you again. (*Turns* R.) And—and I would, if only I could be sure that you would notice I wasn't speaking to you.

WOODCUTTER. After all, I'm just as bad as you. Only yesterday I was thinking to myself how unselfish I was to interrupt my work in order to talk to a mere Princess.

PRINCESS. Yes, but the trouble is that you *don't* interrupt your work.

WOODCUTTER (*interrupting it and going up to her with a smile.*) Madam, I am at your service.

PRINCESS. I wish I thought you were.

WOODCUTTER. Surely you have enough people at your service already. Princes and Chancellors and Chamberlains and Waiting Maids.

PRINCESS. Yes, that's just it. That's why I want your help. Particularly in the matter of Princes.

WOODCUTTER. Why, has a suitor come for the hand of her Royal Highness ?

PRINCESS. Three suitors. And I hate them all.

WOODCUTTER. And which are you going to marry ?

PRINCESS. I don't know. Father hasn't made up his mind yet.

WOODCUTTER. And this is a matter which father—which His Majesty decides for himself ?

PRINCESS. Why, of course ! You should read the History Books, Woodcutter. The suitors to the hand of a Princess are always set some trial of strength or test of quality by the King, and the winner marries his daughter.

WOODCUTTER. Well, I don't live in a Palace, and I think my own thoughts about these things. I'd better get back to my work. (*He goes on with his chopping.*)

PRINCESS (*gently, after a pause*). Woodcutter !

WOODCUTTER (*looking up*). Oh, are you there ? I thought you were married by this time.

PRINCESS (*meekly*). I don't want to be married. (*Hastily.*) I mean, not to any of those three.

WOODCUTTER. You can't help yourself.
PRINCESS. I know. That's why I wanted *you* to help me.
WOODCUTTER (*going up to her*). Can a simple woodcutter help a Princess?
PRINCESS. Well, perhaps a simple one couldn't, but a clever one might.
WOODCUTTER. What would his reward be?
PRINCESS. His reward would be that the Princess, not being married to any of her three suitors, would still be able to help him chop his wood in the mornings. . . . I *am* helping you, aren't I?
WOODCUTTER (*smiling*). Oh, decidedly.
PRINCESS (*nodding*). I thought I was.
WOODCUTTER. It is kind of a great lady like yourself to help so humble a fellow as I.
PRINCESS (*meekly*). I'm not *very* great. (*And she isn't. She is the smallest, daintiest little Princess that ever you saw.*)
WOODCUTTER. There's enough of you to make a hundred men unhappy.
PRINCESS. And one man happy?
WOODCUTTER. And one man very, very happy.
PRINCESS (*innocently*). I wonder who he'll be. . . . Woodcutter, if *you* were a Prince, would you be my suitor?
WOODCUTTER (*scornfully*). One of three?
PRINCESS (*excitedly*). Oo, would you kill the others? With that axe?
WOODCUTTER. I would not kill them, in order to help His Majesty make up his mind about his son-in-law. But if the Princess had made up her mind—and wanted me——
PRINCESS. Yes?
WOODCUTTER. Then I would marry her, however many suitors she had.
PRINCESS. Well, she's only got three at present.
WOODCUTTER. What is that to me?
PRINCESS. Oh, I just thought you might want to be doing something to your axe.
WOODCUTTER. My axe?
PRINCESS. Yes. You see, she *has* made up her mind.
WOODCUTTER (*amazed*). You mean—— But—but I'm only a woodcutter.
PRINCESS. That's where you'll have the advantage of them when it comes to axes.
WOODCUTTER. Princess! (*He takes her in his arms.*) My Princess!
PRINCESS. Woodcutter! My Woodcutter! My, oh so very slow and uncomprehending, but entirely adorable woodcutter!

(*They sing together. They just happen to feel like that.*)

OUR FAIRY STORY.

Duet: WOODCUTTER AND PRINCESS.

PRINCESS. My dear brown man,
With your strength and grace,
And your most attractive face,
Do you wonder how my love for you began?
Well, I don't quite know,
But with those dear arms around me
I know my fate has found me.

WOODCUTTER. My own, fair maid,
With all heaven in your eyes,
Are we mad or truly wise
When the laws of courts and kings are disobeyed?
Let the world go by,
With its pride and pomp and glory,
We have made our fairy story.

BOTH. This is just our fairy story,
Every word of which is true,
Older than the hills around us,
Yet so wonderfully new.
All the stories worth the telling
Surely must be told by two,
Each must have the self-same ending,
"You love me and I love you."

PRINCESS.—My dear, brown man!
Just because I love you blindly
You must rule me very kindly,
For I mean to be obedient—if I can!
I'm a poor spoiled child
And my future education
Will afford you occupation,
But I recognize my master underneath the toiler's tan.

WOODCUTTER. My own, fair maid,
I declare your very meekness
Is the measure of my weakness,
And my mastery will seldom be displayed.
For at one shy glance
From beneath those drooping lashes
All my airy kingship crashes.

BOTH. (As before).

WOODCUTTER (*the song finished*). But what will His Majesty say?

PRINCESS. All sorts of things. . . . Do you really love me, woodcutter, or have I proposed to you under a misapprehension?

WOODCUTTER. I adore you!

PRINCESS (*nodding*). I thought you did. But I wanted to hear you say it. If I had been a simple peasant, I suppose you would have said it a long time ago?

WOODCUTTER. I expect so.

PRINCESS (*nodding*). Yes. . . . Well, now we must think of a plan for making Mother like you.

WOODCUTTER. Might I just kiss you again before we begin?

PRINCESS. Well, I don't quite see how I am to stop you.

(*The* WOODCUTTER *picks her up in his arms and kisses her.*)

WOODCUTTER. There!

PRINCESS (*in his arms*). Oh, woodcutter, woodcutter, why didn't you do that the first day I saw you? Then I needn't have had the bother of proposing to you. (*He puts her down suddenly.*) What is it?

WOODCUTTER (*listening*). Somebody coming. (*He peers through the trees and then says in surprise.*) The King!

PRINCESS. Oh! I must fly!

WOODCUTTER. But you'll come back?

PRINCESS. Perhaps.

(*She disappears quickly through the trees.*)

(*The* WOODCUTTER *goes on with his work and is discovered at it a minute later by the* KING *and* QUEEN. *The music of "Tête à Tête" is played for the entrance. There enter first* 1 *red and* 1 *black attendant, walking backwards and bowing to the* KING *and* QUEEN. *They are followed by two other attendants.*)

KING (*puffing*). Ah! and a seat all ready for us. How satisfying. (*They sit down, a distinguished couple—reading from left to right, "* KING, QUEEN *"—on a bench outside the* WOODCUTTER'S *hut.*)

QUEEN (*crossly—she was like that*). I don't know why you dragged me here.

KING. As I told you, my love, to be alone.

(*All attendants go off.*)

QUEEN. Well, you aren't alone. (*She indicates the* WOODCUTTER.)

KING. Pooh, he doesn't matter. . . . Well now, about these three Princes. They are getting on my mind rather. It is time we decided which one of them is to marry our beloved child. The trouble is to choose between them.

QUEEN. As regards appetite, there is nothing to choose between them. They are three of the heartiest eaters I have met for some time.

KING. You are right. The sooner we choose one of them, and send the other two about their business, the better. (*Reflectively.*) There were six peaches on the breakfast-table this morning. Did I get one? No.

QUEEN. Did *I* get one? No.

KING. Did our darling get one—not that it matters? No.

QUEEN. It is a pity that the seven-headed bull died last year.

KING (*with a sigh*). Those days are over. We must think of a new test. Somehow I think that, in a son-in-law, moral worth is even more to be desired than mere brute strength. Now my suggestion is

Act I.]   MAKE-BELIEVE.   15

this: that you should disguise yourself as a beggar woman and approach each of the three princes in turn, supplicating their charity. In this way we shall discover which of the three has the kindest heart. What do you say, my dear?

QUEEN. An excellent plan. If you remember, I suggested it myself yesterday.

KING (*annoyed*). Well, of course, it had been in my mind for some time. I don't claim that the idea is original; it has often been done in our family. (*Getting up.*) Well then, if you will get ready, my dear, I will go and find our three friends and see that they come this way.

(*They go out together. The music of "Tête à Tête" is played again. As soon as they are out of sight the* PRINCESS *comes back.*)

PRINCESS. Well, Woodcuttter, what did I tell you?
WOODCUTTER. What *did* you tell me?
PRINCESS. Didn't you listen to what they said?
WOODCUTTER. I didn't listen, but I couldn't help hearing.
PRINCESS. Well, *I* couldn't help listening. And unless you stop it somehow, I shall be married to one of them to-night.
WOODCUTTER. Which one?
PRINCESS. The one with the kindest heart—whichever that is.
WOODCUTTER. Supposing they all have kind hearts?
PRINCESS (*confidently*). They won't. They never have. In our circles when three Princes come together, one of them has a kind heart and the other two haven't. (*Surprised.*) Haven't you read any History at all?
WOODCUTTER. I have no time for reading. But I think it's time History was altered a little. We'll alter it this afternoon.
PRINCESS. What do you mean?
WOODCUTTER. Leave this to me. I've got an idea.
PRINCESS (*clapping her hands*). Oh, how clever of you! But what do you want me to do?
WOODCUTTER (*pointing*). You know the glade over there where the brook runs through it? Wait for me there.
PRINCESS. I obey my Lord's commands.

(*She blows him a kiss and runs off.*)

(*The* WOODCUTTER *resumes his work. By and by the* RED PRINCE *comes along. He is a—well, you will see for yourself what he is like.*)

RED PRINCE. Ah, fellow ... Fellow! ... I said fellow! (*Yes, that sort of man.*)
WOODCUTTER (*looking up*). Were you speaking to me, my lord?
RED PRINCE. There is no other fellow here that I can see.

(*The* WOODCUTTER *looks round to make sure, peers behind a tree or two, and comes back to the* PRINCE.)

WOODCUTTER. Yes, you must have meant me.

RED PRINCE. Yes, of course I meant you, fellow. Have you seen the Princess come past this way? I was told she was waiting for me here.

WOODCUTTER. She is not here, my lord. (*Looking round to see that they are alone.*) My lord, are you one of the Princes who is seeking the hand of the Princess.

RED PRINCE (*complacently*). I am, fellow.

WOODCUTTER. His Majesty the King was here awhile ago. He is to make his decision between you this afternoon. (*Meaningly.*) I think I can help you to be the lucky one, my lord.

RED PRINCE. You suggest that I take an unfair advantage over my fellow-competitors?

WOODCUTTER. I suggest nothing, my lord. I only say that I can help you.

RED PRINCE (*magnanimously*). Well, I will allow you to help me.

WOODCUTTER. Thank you. Then I will give you this advice. If a beggar woman asks you for a crust of bread this afternoon, remember—it is the test!

RED PRINCE (*staggered*). The test! But I haven't *got* a crust of bread!

WOODCUTTER. Wait here and I will get you one.

(*He goes into the hut.*)

RED PRINCE (*speaking after him as he goes*). My good fellow, I am extremely obliged to you, and if ever I can do anything for you, such as returning a crust to you of similar size, or even lending you another slightly smaller one, or——(*The* WOODCUTTER *comes back with the crust.*) Ah, thank you, my man, thank you.

WOODCUTTER. I would suggest, my lord, that you should take a short walk in this direction (*pointing to the opposite direction to that which the* PRINCESS *has taken*), and stroll back casually in a few minutes' time when the Queen is here.

RED PRINCE. Thank you, my man, thank you.

(*He puts the crust in his pocket and goes off.*)

(*The* WOODCUTTER *goes on with his work. The* BLUE PRINCE *comes in and stands watching him in silence for some moments.*)

WOODCUTTER (*looking up*). Hullo!
BLUE PRINCE. Hullo!
WOODCUTTER. What do you want?
BLUE PRINCE. The Princess.
WOODCUTTER. She's not here.
BLUE PRINCE. Oh!

(*The* WOODCUTTER *goes on with his work and the* PRINCE *goes on looking at him.*)

WOODCUTTER (*struck with an idea*). Are you one of the Princes who is wooing the Princess?

BLUE PRINCE. Yes.
WOODCUTTER (*coming towards him*). I believe I could help your Royal Highness.
BLUE PRINCE. Do.
WOODCUTTER (*doubtfully*). It would perhaps be not quite fair to the others.
BLUE PRINCE. Don't mind.
WOODCUTTER. Well then, listen. (*He pauses a moment and looks round to see that they are alone.*)
BLUE PRINCE. I'm listening.
WOODCUTTER. If you come back in five minutes, you will see a beggar woman sitting here. She will ask you for a crust of bread. You must give it to her, for it is the way His Majesty has chosen of testing your kindness of heart.
BLUE PRINCE (*feeling in his pockets*). No bread.
WOODCUTTER. I will give you some.
BLUE PRINCE. Do.
WOODCUTTER (*taking a piece from his pocket*). Here you are.
BLUE PRINCE. Thanks.
WOODCUTTER. Not at all, I'm very glad to have been able to help you.
(*He goes on with his work. The* BLUE PRINCE *remains looking at him.*)

BLUE PRINCE (*with a great effort*). Thanks.

(*He goes slowly away. A moment later the* YELLOW PRINCE *makes a graceful and languid entry.*)

YELLOW PRINCE. Ah, come hither, my man, come hither.
WOODCUTTER (*stopping his work and looking up*). You want me, sir?
YELLOW PRINCE. Come hither, my man. Tell me, has her Royal Highness the Princess passed this way lately?
WOODCUTTER. The Princess?
YELLOW PRINCE (*slaps* WOODCUTTER'S *shoulder*). Yes, the Princess, my bumpkin. But perhaps you have been too much concerned in your own earthly affairs to have noticed her. You—ah—cut wood, I see.
WOODCUTTER. Yes, sir, I am a woodcutter.
YELLOW PRINCE. A most absorbing life. Some day we must have a long talk about it. But just now I have other business waiting for me. With your permission, good friend, I will leave you to your faggots. (*He starts to go.*)
WOODCUTTER. Beg your pardon, sir, but are you one of those Princes that want to marry our Princess?
YELLOW PRINCE. I had hoped, good friend, to obtain your permission to do so. I beg you not to refuse it.
WOODCUTTER. You are making fun of me, sir.
YELLOW PRINCE. Discerning creature.

WOODCUTTER. All the same, I *can* help you.

YELLOW PRINCE. Then pray do so, log-chopper, and earn my everlasting gratitude.

WOODCUTTER. The King has decided that whichever of you three Princes has the kindest heart shall marry his daughter.

YELLOW PRINCE. Then you will be able to bear witness to him that I have already wasted several minutes of my valuable time in condescending to a mere faggot-splitter. Tell him this and the prize is mine. (*Kissing the tips of his fingers.*) Princess, I embrace you.

WOODCUTTER. The King will not listen to me. But if you return here in five minutes, you will find an old woman begging for bread. It is the test which their Majesties have arranged for you. If you share your last crust with her——

YELLOW PRINCE. Yes, but do I look as if I carried a last crust about with me?

WOODCUTTER. But see, I will give you one.

YELLOW PRINCE (*taking it between the tips of his fingers*). Yes, but——

WOODCUTTER. Put it in your pocket, and when——

YELLOW PRINCE. But, my dear bark-scraper, have you no feeling for clothes at all? How can I put a thing like this in my pocket? (*Handing it back to him.*) I beg you to wrap it up. Here take this. (*Gives him a scarf.*) Neatly, I pray you. (*Taking an orange ribbon out of his pocket.*) Perhaps a little of this round it would make it more tolerable. You think so? I leave it to you. I trust your taste entirely. . . . Leaving a loop for the little finger, I entreat you . . . so. (*He hangs it on his little finger.*) In about five minutes, you said? We will be there. (*With a bow.*) We thank you.

(*He departs delicately. The* WOODCUTTER *smiles to himself, puts down his axe and goes off to the* PRINCESS. *And just in time. For behold! the* KING *and* QUEEN *return. The same music as before. At least we think it is the* QUEEN, *but she is so heavily disguised by a cloak which she wears over her court dress, that for a moment we are not quite sure.*)

KING. Now then, my love, if you will sit down on that log there —(*placing her*)—excellent—I think perhaps you should remove the crown. (*Removes it.*) There! Now the disguise is perfect.

QUEEN. You're sure they are coming? It's a very uncomfortable seat. (*Takes out long nail.*)

KING. I told them that the Princess was waiting for them here. Their natural disappointment at finding I was mistaken will make the test of their good nature an even more exacting one. My own impression is that the Yellow Prince will be the victor.

QUEEN. Oh, I hate that man.

KING (*soothingly*). Well, well, perhaps it will be the Blue one.

QUEEN. If anything, I dislike him *more* intensely.

KING. Or even the Red.

QUEEN. Ugh! I can't bear him.

KING. Fortunately, dear, you are not called upon to marry any of them. It is for our darling that we are making the great decision. Listen! I hear one coming. I will hide in the cottage and take note of what happens.

(*He disappears into the cottage as the* BLUE PRINCE *comes in.*)

QUEEN. Oh, sir, can you kindly spare a crust of bread for a poor old woman! Please, pretty gentleman!

BLUE PRINCE (*standing stolidly in front of her and feeling in his pocket*). Bread . . . Bread . . . Ah! Bread! (*He offers it.*)

QUEEN. Oh, thank you, sir. May you be rewarded for your gentle heart.

BLUE PRINCE. Thank you.

(*He stands gazing at her. There is an awkward pause.*)

QUEEN. A blessing on you, sir.

BLUE PRINCE. Thank you. (*He indicates the crust.*) Bread.

QUEEN. Ah, you have saved the life of a poor old woman——

BLUE PRINCE. Eat it.

QUEEN (*embarrassed*). I—er—you—er—— (*She takes a bite and mumbles something.*)

BLUE PRINCE. What?

QUEEN (*swallowing with great difficulty*). I'm almost too happy to eat, sir. Leave a poor old woman alone with her happiness, and——

BLUE PRINCE. Not too happy. Too weak. Help you eat. (*He breaks off a piece and holds it to her mouth. With a great effort the* QUEEN *disposes of it.*) Good! . . . Again! (*She does it again.*) Now! (*She swallows another piece.*) Last piece! (*She takes it in. He pats her kindly on the back, and she nearly chokes.*) Good. . . . Better now?

QUEEN (*weakly*). Much.

BLUE PRINCE. Good day.

QUEEN (*with an effort*). Good day, kind gentleman.

(*He goes out.*)

(*The* KING *is just coming from the cottage, when he returns suddenly. The* KING *slips back again.*)

BLUE PRINCE. Small piece left over. (*He gives it to her. She looks hopelessly at him.*) Good-bye.

(*He goes.*)

QUEEN (*throwing the piece down violently*). Ugh! What a man!

KING (*coming out*). Well, well, my dear, we have discovered the winner.

QUEEN (*from the heart*). Detestable person!

KING. The rest of the competition is of course more in the nature of a formality——

QUEEN. Thank goodness.

KING. However, I think that it will prevent unnecessary discussion afterwards if we—— Take care, here is another one. (*He hurries back.*)

(*Enter the* RED PRINCE.)

QUEEN (*with not nearly so much conviction*). Could you spare a crust of bread, sir, for a poor hungry old woman?

RED PRINCE. A crust of bread, madam? Certainly. As luck will have it, I have a crust on me. My last one, but—your need is greater than mine. Eat, I pray.

QUEEN. Th-thank you, sir.

RED PRINCE. Not at all. Come, eat. Let me have the pleasure of seeing you eating.

QUEEN. M-might I take it home with me, pretty gentleman?

RED PRINCE (*firmly*). No, no. I must see you eating. Come! I will take no denial.

QUEEN. Th-thank you, sir. (*Hopefully.*) Won't you share it with me?

RED PRINCE. No, I insist on your having it all. I am in the mood to be generous. Oblige me by eating it now, for I am in a hurry; yet I will not go until you have eaten. (*She does her best.*) You eat but slowly. (*Sternly.*) Did you deceive me when you said you were hungry?

QUEEN. N-no. I'm very hungry. (*She eats.*)

RED PRINCE. That's better. Now understand—however poor I am, I can always find a crust of bread for an old woman. Always! Remember this when next you are hungry. . . . You spoke? (*She shakes her head and goes on eating.*) Finished?

QUEEN (*with great difficulty*). Yes, thank you, pretty gentleman.

RED PRINCE. There's a piece on the ground there that you dropped. (*She eats it in dumb agony.*) Finished?

QUEEN (*huskily*). Yes, thank you, pretty gentleman.

RED PRINCE. Then I will leave you, madam. Good morning.

(*He goes out.*)

(*The* QUEEN *rises in fury. The* KING *is about to come out of the cottage, when the* YELLOW PRINCE *enters. The* QUEEN *sits down again and mumbles something. It is certainly not an appeal for bread, but the* YELLOW PRINCE *is not to be denied.*)

YELLOW PRINCE (*gallantly*). My poor woman, you are in distress. It pains me to see it, madam, it pains me terribly. Can it be that you are hungry? I thought so, I thought so. Give me the great pleasure, madam, of relieving your hunger. See (*holding up his finger*) my own poor meal. Take it! It is yours.

QUEEN (*with difficulty*). I am not hungry.

YELLOW PRINCE. Ah, madam, I see what it is. You do not wish

to deprive me. You tell yourself, perchance, that it is not fitting that one in your station of life should partake of the meals of the highly born. You are not used, you say, to the food of Princes. Your rougher palate——

QUEEN (*hopefully*). Did you say food of princes?

YELLOW PRINCE. Where was I, madam? You interrupted me. No matter—eat. (*She takes the scarf and unties the ribbon.*) Ah, now I remember. I was saying that your rougher palate——

QUEEN (*discovering the worst*). No! No! Not bread!

YELLOW PRINCE. Bread, madam, the staff of life. Come, madam, will you not eat? (*She tries desperately.*) What can be more delightful than a crust of bread by the wayside?

(*The* QUEEN *shrieks and falls back in a swoon. The* KING *rushes out to her.*)

KING (*to* YELLOW PRINCE). Quick, quick, find the Princess.

YELLOW PRINCE. The Princess—find the Princess!

(*He goes vaguely off and we shall not see him again. But the* WOODCUTTER *and the* PRINCESS *do not need to be found. They are here.*)

WOODCUTTER (*to* PRINCESS). Go to her, but don't show that you know me.

(*He goes into the cottage, and the* PRINCESS *hastens to her father.*)

PRINCESS. Father!

KING. Ah, my dear, you're just in time. Your mother——

PRINCESS. My mother?

KING. Yes, yes. A little plan of mine—of hers—your poor mother. Dear, dear!

PRINCESS. But what's the matter?

KING. She is suffering from a surfeit of bread, and——

(*The* WOODCUTTER *comes up with a flagon of wine.*)

WOODCUTTER. Poor old woman! She has fainted from exhaustion. Let me give her some——

QUEEN (*shrieking*). No, no, not bread! I will *not* have any more bread.

WOODCUTTER. Drink this, my poor woman.

QUEEN (*opening her eyes*). Did you say drink? (*She seizes the flagon and drinks.*)

PRINCESS. Oh, sir, you have saved my mother's life!

WOODCUTTER. Not at all.

KING. I thank you, my man, I thank you.

QUEEN (*goes to* WOODCUTTER *and flings her arms round him*). My deliverer! Tell me who you are!

PRINCESS. It is my mother, the Queen, who asks you.

WOODCUTTER (*amazed, as well he may be*). The Queen! (*Kneels and covers his face.*)

King. Yes, yes. Certainly, the Queen.

Woodcutter (*taking off his hat*). Pardon, your Majesty. I am a woodcutter, who lives alone here, far away from courts.

Queen. Well, you've got more sense in your head than any of the Princes that *I've* seen lately. You'd better come to court.

Princess (*shyly*). You will be very welcome, sir.

Queen. And you'd better marry the Princess.

King. Isn't that perhaps going a *little* too far, dear ?

Queen. Well, you wanted kindness of heart in your son-in-law, and you've got it. And he's got common sense too. (*To* Woodcutter.) Tell me, what do you think of bread as—as a form of nourishment ?

Woodcutter (*cautiously*). One can have too much of it.

Queen. Exactly my view. (*To* King.) There you are, you see.

King. Well, if you insist. The great thing, of course, is that our darling child should be happy.

Princess. I will do my best, father. (*She takes the* Woodcutter's *hand.*)

King. Then the marriage will take place this evening. (*With a wave of his wand.*) Let the revels begin.

(*They begin.*)

(*Children dance. The refrain of the "Fairy Story" song is used. See pages 18 and 19 in the score.*)

(*The* King *and* Queen *go off and the* Curtain *falls.*)

End of Act I.

ACT II

Oliver's Island.

Scene I.—*The Schoolroom* (*Ugh !*)

Oliver *is discovered lying flat on his—well, lying flat on the floor, deep in a book. The* Curate *puts his head in at the door.*)

Curate. Ah, our young friend, Oliver! And how are we this morning, dear lad?

Oliver (*mumbling*). All right, thanks.

Curate. That's well, that's well. (*Takes a step forward.*) Deep in our studies, I see, deep in our studies. (*Takes another step forward.*) And what branch of Knowledge are we pursuing this morning?

Oliver (*without looking up*). "Marooned in the Pacific," or "The Pirate's Bride."

Curate. Dear, dear, what will Miss Pinniger say to this interruption of our studies?

Oliver. Silly old beast.

Curate. Tut-tut, dear lad, that is not the way to speak of our mentors and preceptors. So refined and intelligent a lady as Miss Pinniger. Indeed I came here to see her this morning on a little matter of embroidered vestments. Where is she, dear lad?

Oliver. It isn't nine yet.

Curate (*looking at his watch*). Past nine, past nine.

Oliver (*jumping up*). Je-hosaphat!

Curate. Oliver! Oliver! My dear lad! Swearing at *your* age! Really, I almost feel it my duty to inform your aunt——

Oliver. Fat lot of swearing in just mentioning one of the kings of Israel.

Curate. Of Judah, dear boy, of Judah. To be ignorant on such a vital matter makes it even more reprehensible. I cannot believe that our dear Miss Pinniger has so neglected your education that——

(*Enter our dear* Miss Pinniger, *the Governess.*)

Governess. Ah, Mr. Smilax; how pleasant to see you!

Curate. My dear Miss Pinniger! You will forgive me for interrupting you in your labours, but there is a small matter of—ah!——

Governess. Certainly, Mr. Smilax. I will walk down to the gate with you. Oliver, where is Geraldine?

OLIVER. Aunt Jane wanted her.
GOVERNESS. Well, you should be at your lessons. It's nine o'clock. The fact that I am momentarily absent from the room should make no difference to your zeal.
OLIVER (*without conviction*). No, Miss Pinniger. (*He sits down at his desk, putting " Marooned in the Pacific " inside it.*)
CURATE (*playfully*). For men must work, Oliver, men must work. How doth the little busy bee—— Yes, Miss Pinniger, I am with you.

(*They go out.*)

OLIVER (*opening his poetry book and saying it to himself*). It was a summer evening—It was a summer evening—(*He stops, refers to the book, and then goes on to himself.*) Old Kaspar's work was done. It was a summer evening, Old Kaspar's work was done——

(*Enter* GERALDINE—*or* JILL.)

JILL. Where's Pin?
OLIVER. Hallo, Jill. Gone off with Dearly Belovéd. Her momentary absence from the room should make no difference to your zeal, my dear Geraldine. And what are we studying this morning, dear child? (*To himself.*) It was a summer evening, Old Kaspar's work was done.
JILL. (*giggling*). Is that Pin?
OLIVER. Pin and Dearly Belovéd between them. She's a bit batey this morning.
JILL (*at her desk*). And all my sums have done themselves wrong. (*Hard at it with paper and pencil.*) What's nine times seven, Oliver?
OLIVER. Fifty-six. Old Kaspar's work was done. Jolly well wish mine was. And he before his cottage door. Fat lot of good my learning this stuff if I'm going to be a sailor. I bet Beatty didn't mind what happened to rotten old Kaspar when he saw a German submarine.
JILL. Six and carry five. Aunt Jane has sent for the doctor to look at my chest.
OLIVER. What's the matter with your chest?
JILL. I blew my nose rather loud at prayers this morning.
OLIVER. I say, Jill, you *are* going it!
JILL. It wasn't my fault, Oliver. Aunt Jane turned over two pages at once and made me laugh, so I had to turn it into a blow.
OLIVER. Bet you what you like she knew.
JILL. Of course she did, and she'll tell the doctor, and he'll be as beastly as he can. What did she say to you for being late?
OLIVER. I said somebody had bagged my sponge, and she wouldn't like me to come down to prayers all unsponged, and she said, "Excuses, Oliver, *always* excuses! Leave me. I will see you later." Suppose that means I've got to go to bed this afternoon. Jill, if I do, be sporty and bring me up " Marooned in the Pacific."

Jill. They'll lock the door. They always do.

Oliver. Then I shall jolly well go up for a handkerchief this morning, and shove it in the bed, just in case. Cave—here's Pin.

(Miss Pinniger *returns to find them full of zeal*.)

Governess (*sitting down at her desk*). Well, Oliver, have you learnt your piece of poetry?

Oliver (*nervously*). I—I think so, Miss Pinniger.

Governess. Close the book, and stand up and say it. (Oliver *takes a last despairing look, and stands up*.) Well?

Oliver. It was a summer evening——

Governess. The title and the author first, Oliver. Everything in its proper order.

Oliver. Oh, I say, I didn't know I had to learn the title.

Jill (*in a whisper*). After Blenheim.

Governess. Geraldine, kindly attend to your own work.

Oliver. After Blenheim. It was a summer evening.

Governess. After Blenheim, by Robert Southey. One of our greatest poets.

Oliver. After Blenheim, by Robert Southey, one of our greatest poets. It was a summer evening, Old Kaspar's work was done —er—Old Kaspar's work was done—er—work was done, er . . .

Governess. And he before——

Oliver. Oh yes, of course. And he before—er—and he before —er—It was a summer evening, Old Kaspar's work was done, and he before—er—and he before—— Er, it *was* a summer evening——

Governess. So you have already said, Oliver.

Oliver. I just seem to have forgotten this bit, Miss Pinniger. And he before——

Governess. Well, what was he before?

Oliver (*hopefully*). Blenheim? Oh no, it was *after* Blenheim.

Governess (*wearily*). His cottage door.

Oliver. Oo, yes. And he before his cottage door was sitting in the sun. (*He clears his throat*.) Was sitting in the sun. Er— (*he coughs again*)—er——

Governess. You have a cough, Oliver. Perhaps the doctor had better see you when he comes to see Geraldine.

Oliver. It was just something tickling my throat, Miss Pinniger. Er—it was a summer evening.

Governess. You haven't learnt it, Oliver?

Oliver. Yes, I have, Miss Pinniger, only I can't quite remember it. And he before his cottage door— -

Governess. Is it any good, Geraldine, asking you if you have got any of your sums right?

Jill. I've got one, Miss Pinniger . . . nearly right . . . except for some of the figures.

Governess. Well, we shall have to spend more time at our lessons, that's all. This afternoon—ah—er——

EDUCATION.

Trio : GOVERNESS, OLIVER *and* JILL.)

GOVERNESS. Now, children, pay
Attention pray
To what I am about to say;
I wish to cure you, if I may,
Of idle careless habits.
I must confess
You much distress
Your kind and thoughtful governess,
Because I fear you scarce possess
The intellect of rabbits.
Each little brain,
'Tis very plain,
Must learn, and learn, and learn again
If it's going to retain
The simplest proposition.
But though 'tis true
Each day that you
Forget what yesterday you knew
I mean to see what we can do
With constant repetition.

OLIVER *and* JILL. The rivers of England, if you please,
Are the Thames, the Thine, the Tear, and the Wheeze,
York is the largest seaside town,
And pillows are made in County Down.
When good King John by a peach was slain
It is said that he never smiled again :
Fresh butter is sold by the pat,
And Shah is the French for a Persian cat.

GOVERNESS. Upon my word,
I never heard
A string of statements so absurd!
I warn you that you have incurred
My very keen displeasure.
You always shirk
The tasks that irk,
Which means an extra dose of work,
For now we see what dangers lurk
In too long hours of leisure.
I do declare
I quite despair ;
To think of all the loving care
That I have spent upon a pair
So mentally defective.
No use to cry
And rub your eye,
I cannot pass such conduct by.
Proceed at once or I must try
A suitable corrective,
Proceed at once or I must try
A suitable corrective.

OLIVER *and* JILL. Thirty hundredweight make a ton
With seventeen over and carry one,
A decimal point is a thing so small
It is less than a tenth of nothing at all;

MAKE-BELIEVE.

Hamlet, a prince of Elizabeth's days
Was poisoned for writing Bacon's plays;
And Sir Isaac Newton was killed stone dead
By an apple which fell on his bald old head.

OMNES. Education! Education!
You are nothing but vexation.
Stupid pupil, harassed teacher,
Each is an unhappy creature.
Source of gloom and desperation,
Education! Education!

(*During the song, both children stand up. The* GOVERNESS *stands at the finish for the entrance of* AUNT JANE *and the* DOCTOR.)

AUNT JANE. I'm sorry to interrupt lessons, Miss Pinniger, but I have brought the Doctor to see Geraldine. (*To* DOCTOR.) You will like her to go to her room?

DOCTOR. No, no, dear lady. There is no need. Her pulse—(*he feels it*)—dear, dear! Her tongue—(*she puts it out*)—tut-tut! A milk diet, plenty of rice-pudding, and perhaps she would do well to go to bed this afternoon.

AUNT JANE. I will see to it, doctor.

JILL (*mutinously*). I *feel* quite well.

DOCTOR (*to* AUNT JANE). A dangerous symptom. *Plenty* of rice-pudding.

GOVERNESS. Oliver was coughing just now.

OLIVER (*to himself*). Shut up!

DOCTOR (*turning to* OLIVER). Ah! His pulse—(*feels it*)—tut-tut! His tongue—(OLIVER *puts it out.*) Dear, dear! The same treatment, dear lady, as prescribed in the other case.

OLIVER (*under his breath*). Beast!

AUNT JANE. Castor oil, liquorice powder, ammoniated quinine —anything of that nature, doctor?

DOCTOR. *As* necessary, dear lady, *as* necessary. The system must be stimulated. Nature must be reinforced.

AUNT JANE (*to* GOVERNESS). Which do they dislike least?

OLIVER *and* JILL (*hastily*). Liquorice-powder!

DOCTOR. Then concentrate on the other two, dear lady.

AUNT JANE. Thank you, doctor.

(*They go out.*)

GOVERNESS. We will now resume our lessons. Oliver, give me that book which you were reading when I came in just now.

OLIVER (*trying to be surprised*). Which book?

JILL (*nobly doing her best to save the situation*). Miss Pinniger, if you're multiplying rods, poles, or perches, by nine, does it matter if—— (*Going up to* MISS PINNIGER *with her work.*) You see, it's all gone wrong here, and I think I must have multiplied—— (*Moving in front of her as she moves.*) I think I must have multiplied——

(*Under cover of this,* OLIVER *makes a great effort to get the book into* JILL'S *desk, but it is no good.*)

GOVERNESS (*brushing aside* JILL *and advancing on* OLIVER). Thank you, *I* will take it.

OLIVER (*looking at the title*). Oh yes, this is the one.

GOVERNESS. And I will speak to your aunt at *once* about the behaviour of both of you.

(*She goes out.*)

OLIVER (*gallantly*). *I* don't care.

JILL. I did try to help you, Oliver.

OLIVER. You wait. Won't I jolly well bag something of hers one day, just when she wants it.

JILL. I'm afraid you'll find the afternoon rather tiring without your book. What will you do?

OLIVER. I suppose I shall have to think.

JILL. What shall you think about?

OLIVER. I shall think I'm on my desert island.

JILL. Which desert island?

OLIVER. The one I always pretend I'm on when I'm thinking.

JILL. Isn't there anyone else on it ever?

OLIVER. Oo, lots of pirates and Dyaks and cannibals and—other people.

JILL. What sort of other people?

OLIVER. I shan't tell you. This is a special think I thought last night. As soon as I thought of it, I decided to keep it for (*impressively*) a moment of great emergency.

JILL (*silenced*). Oh! . . . Oliver?

OLIVER. Yes?

JILL. Let me be on your desert island this time. Because I did try to help you.

OLIVER. Well—well—— (*Generously.*) Well, you can if you like. (*Sits on floor.*)

JILL. Oh, thank you, Oliver. Won't you tell me what it's about, and then we can both think it together this afternoon.

OLIVER. I expect you'll think all sorts of silly things that *never* happen on a desert island.

JILL. I'll try not to, Oliver, if you tell me.

OLIVER. All right.

JILL (*coming close to him*). Go on.

OLIVER. Well, you see, I've been wrecked, you see, and the ship has foundered with all hands, you see, and I've been cast ashore on a desert island, you see.

JILL. Haven't I been cast ashore too?

OLIVER. Well, you will be this afternoon, of course. Well, you see, we land on the island, you see, and it's a perfectly ripping island, you see, and—and we land on it, you see, and . . .

. . . .

But we are getting on too fast. When the good ship crashed upon the rock and split in twain, it seemed like that all aboard must perish.

Act II.] MAKE-BELIEVE. 29

Fortunately OLIVER *was made of stern mettle. Hastily constructing a raft and placing the now unconscious* JILL *upon it, he launched it into the seething maelstrom of waters and pushed off. Tossed like a cockleshell upon the mountainous waves, the tiny craft with its precious freight was in imminent danger of foundering. But* OLIVER *was made of stern mettle. With dauntless courage he rigged a jury-mast, and placed a telescope to his eye.* " *Pull for the lagoon,* JILL," *cried the dauntless* OLIVER, *and in another moment* . . .

As the raft glides into the still waters beyond the reef, we can see it more clearly. Can it be JILL'S *bed, with* OLIVER *in his pyjamas perched on the rail, and holding up his bath-towel ? Does he shorten sail for a moment to thump his chest and say,* " *But* OLIVER *was made of stern mettle ?* " *Or is it——*

But the sun is sinking behind the swamp where the rattlesnakes bask. For a moment the sail gleams like copper in its rays, and then —fizz-z—we have lost it. See! Is that speck on the inky black water the dauntless OLIVER *? It is. Let us follow to the island and see what adventures befall him.*

SCENE II.—*It is the island which we have dreamed about all our lives. But at present we cannot see it properly, for it is dark.*

(*Here comes the* " *Dance of the Firefly.*")

In one of those tropical darknesses which can be felt rather than seen OLIVER *hands* JILL *out of the boat.*

OLIVER. Tread carefully, Jill, there are lots of deadly rattlesnakes about.

JILL (*stepping hastily back into the boat*). Oli-ver!

OLIVER. You hear the noise of their rattles sometimes when the sun is sinking behind the swamp. (*The deadly rattle of the rattlesnake is heard.*) There!

JILL. Oh, Oliver, are they very deadly? Because if they are, I don't think I shall like your island.

OLIVER. Those aren't. I always have their teeth taken out when ladies are coming. Besides, it will be daylight in a minute.

(*With a rapidity common in the tropics—although it may just be* OLIVER'S *gallantry—the sun climbs out of the sea, and floods the island.* JILL, *no longer frightened, steps out of the boat, and they walk up to the clearing in the middle.*)

JILL (*looking about her*). Oh, what a lovely island! I think it's lovely, Oliver.

OLIVER (*modestly*). It's pretty decent, isn't it? Won't you lie down? I generally lie down here and watch the turtles coming out of the sea to deposit their eggs on the sand.

JILL (*lying down*). How many do they de-deposit usually, Oliver?
OLIVER. Oh, three—or a hundred. Just depends how hungry I am. Have a bull's-eye, won't you?
JILL (*excitedly*). Oh, did you bring some?
OLIVER (*annoyed*). Bring some? (*Brightening up.*) Oh, you mean from the wreck?
JILL (*hastily*). Yes, from the wreck. I mean besides the axe and the bag of nails and the gunpowder.
OLIVER. Couldn't. The ship sank with all hands before I could get them. But it doesn't matter, because (*going up to one of the trees*) I recognize this as the bull's-eye tree. (*He picks a couple of bull's eyes and gives one to her.*)
JILL. Oh, Oliver, how lovely! Thank you. (*She puts it in her mouth.*)
OLIVER (*sucking hard*). There was nothing but bread-fruit trees here the first time I was marooned on it. Rotten things to have on a decent island. So I planted a bull's-eye tree, and a barley-sugar-cane grove, and one or two other things, and made a jolly ripping place of it.
JILL (*pointing*). What's that tree over there?
OLIVER. That one? Rice-pudding tree.
JILL (*getting up indignantly*). Oliver! Take me back to the boat at once.
OLIVER. I say, shut up, Jill. You didn't think I meant it for *you*, did you?
JILL. But there's only you and me on the island.
OLIVER. What about the domestic animals? I suppose *they*'ve got to eat.
JILL. Oh, how lovely! Have we got a goat and a parrot, and —a—a—
OLIVER. Much better than that. Look in that cage there.
JILL. Oh, is that a cage? I never noticed it. What do I do?
OLIVER (*going to it*). Here, I'll show you. (*He draws the blind and the* DOCTOR *is exposed sitting on a stump of wood and blinking at the sudden light.*) What do you think of that?
JILL. Oliver!
OLIVER (*proudly*). I thought of that in bed one night. Spiffing idea, isn't it? I've got some other ones in the plantation over there. Awfully good specimens. I feed 'em on rice-pudding.
JILL. Can this one talk?
OLIVER. I'm teaching it. (*Stirring it up with a stick.*) Come up there.
DOCTOR (*mumbling*). Ninety-nine, ninety-nine . . .
OLIVER. That's all it can say at present. I'm going to give it a swim in the lagoon to-morrow. I want to see if there are any sharks. If there aren't, then we can bathe there afterwards.

(*The* DOCTOR *shudders.*)

JILL. Have you given it a name yet? I think I should like to call it Fluffkins.
OLIVER. Righto! Good night, Fluffkins. Time little doctors were in bed. (*He pulls down the blind.*)
JILL (*lying down again*). Well, I think it's a lovely island.
OLIVER (*lying beside her*). If there's anything you want, you know, you've only got to say so. Pirates or anything like that. There's a ginger-beer well if you're thirsty.
JILL (*closing her eyes*). I'm quite happy, Oliver, thank you.
OLIVER (*after a pause, a little awkwardly*). Jill, you didn't ever want to marry a pirate, did you?
JILL (*still on her back with her eyes shut*). I hadn't thought about it much, Oliver dear.
OLIVER. Because I can get you an awfully decent pirate, if you like, and if I was his brother-in-law it would be ripping. I've often been marooned with him, of course, but never as his brother-in-law.
JILL. Why don't you marry his daughter and be his son-in-law?
OLIVER. He hasn't got a daughter.
JILL. Well, you could think him one.
OLIVER. I don't want to. If ever I'm such a silly ass as to marry, which I'm jolly well not going to be, I shall marry a—a dusky maiden. Jill, be sporty. All girls have to get married some time. It's different with men.
JILL. Very well, Oliver. I don't want to spoil your afternoon.
OLIVER. Good biz. (*He stands up, shuts his eyes and waves his hands about.*) You watch while I signal. (*Squeals like a train signal.*)

(*Enter the* PIRATE CHIEF. *A chord of music.*)

PIRATE CHIEF (*with a flourish*). Gentles, your servant. Commodore Crookshank, at your service. Better known on the Spanish Main as One-eared Eric.
OLIVER. Glad to meet you, Commodore. I'm—er—Two-toed Thomas, the Terror of the Dyaks. But you may call me Oliver, if you like. This is my sister Jill—the Pride of the Pampas.
PIRATE CHIEF (*with another bow*). Charmed!
JILL (*politely*). Don't mention it, Commodore.
OLIVER. My sister wants to marry you. Er—carry on. (*He moves a little away from them and lies down.*)
JILL (*sitting down and indicating a place beside her*). Won't you sit down, Commodore?
PIRATE CHIEF. Thank you, madam. The other side if I may. I shall hear better if you condescend to accept me. (*He sits down on the other side of her.*)
JILL. Oh, I'm so sorry! I was forgetting about your ear.
PIRATE CHIEF. Don't mention it. A little discussion in the La Plata river with a Spanish gentleman. At the end of it I was an ear

short and he was a head short. It was considered in the family that I had won.

(*There is an awkward pause.*)

JILL (*shyly*). Well, Commodore?
PIRATE CHIEF. Won't you call me Eric?
JILL. I am waiting, Eric.
PIRATE CHIEF. Madam, I am not a marrying man, not to any extent, but if you would care to be Mrs. Crookshank, I'd undertake on my part to have the deck swabbed every morning, and to put a polish on the four-pounder that you could see your pretty face in.
JILL. Eric, how sweet of you. But I think you must speak to my brother in the library first. Oli-ver!
OLIVER (*coming up*). Hallo! Settled it?
JILL. It's all settled, Oliver, between Eric and myself, but you will want to ask him about his prospects, won't you?
OLIVER. Yes, yes, of course.
PIRATE. I shall be very glad to tell you anything I can, sir. I think I may say that I am doing fairly well in my profession.
OLIVER. What's your ship? A sloop or a frigate?
PIRATE. A brigantine.
JILL (*excited*). Oh, that's what Oliver puts on his hair when he goes to a party.
OLIVER (*annoyed*). Shut up, Jill! A brigantine? Ah, yes, a rakish craft, eh, Commodore?
PIRATE (*earnestly*). Extremely rakish.
OLIVER. And how many pieces of eight have you?
PIRATE. Nine thousand.
OLIVER. Ah! (*To* JILL.) What's nine times eight?
JILL (*to herself*). Nine times eight.
OLIVER (*to himself*). Nine times eight.
PIRATE (*to himself*). Nine times eight.
JILL. Seventy-two.
PIRATE. I made it seventy-one, but I expect you're right.
OLIVER. Then you've seventy-two thousand pieces altogether?
PIRATE. Yes, sir, about that.
OLIVER. Any doubloons?
PIRATE. Hundreds of 'em.
OLIVER. Ingots of gold?
PIRATE. Lashings of 'em.
JILL. And he's going to polish up the four-pounder until I can see my face in it.
OLIVER. I was just going to ask you about your guns. You've got 'em fore and aft of course?
PIRATE. Yes, sir. A four-pounder fore and a half-pounder haft.
OLIVER (*a little embarrassed*). And do you ever have brothers-in-law in your ship?

PIRATE. Well, I never have had yet, but I have always been looking about for one.

JILL. Oh, Oliver, isn't Eric a *nice* man?

OLIVER (*casually*). I suppose the captain's brother-in-law is generally the first man to board the Spaniard with his cutlass between his teeth?

PIRATE. You might almost say always. Many a ship on the Spanish Main I've had to leave unboarded through want of a brother-in-law. They're touchy about it somehow. Unless the captain's brother-in-law comes first they get complaining.

OLIVER (*bashfully*). And there's just one other thing. If the brigantine happened to put in at an island for water, and the captain's brother-in-law happened—just happened—to be a silly ass and go and marry a dusky maiden, whom he met on the beach——

PIRATE. Bless you, it's always happening to a captain's brother-in-law.

OLIVER (*in a magnificent manner*). Then, Captain Crookshank, you may take my sister!

JILL. Thank you, Oliver.

(*It is not every day that one-eared* ERIC, *that famous chieftain, marries into the family of the* TERROR OF THE DYAKS. *Naturally the occasion is celebrated by the whole pirate crew with a rousing chorus, followed by a dance in which the dusky maidens of the Island join.*)

PIRATE. Would'st hear my pirates warble?
JILL. We wouldst.

(PIRATE *claps hands. Enter* 1ST PIRATE, *who bows.*)

PIRATE. We would hear warbling.
1ST PIRATE. We will warble.

(PIRATES *enter.*)

PIRATE (*introducing*). Let me introduce you to my pirates, Mr. Oliver, Miss Jill. Cecil, Basil, Percy, Archibald, Mervin, Francis, Aloisis, Eglantine.

(*Each* PIRATE *replies* "Pleased to meet you.")

PIECES OF EIGHT.

(*Song :* PIRATE CHIEF *and* CHORUS OF PIRATES.)

CHIEF. Yo Ho Ho! and a bottle of rum,
Under the bold black flag we come,
Each of us worth a tidy sum
In pieces of eight.

Chorus : In pieces of eight.

CHIEF. Silver or copper for those who gain
A landlubber's living in toil and pain,
But for those who harry the Spanish Main,
Pieces of eight.

Chorus : Pieces of eight.

Chorus: Buried deep in the dark of the moon
By the haunted shore of the black lagoon,
And marked in blood on a parchment chart
That every one of us knows by heart,
Snug in their coffers they lie and wait
Pieces of eight. Pieces of eight.

CHIEF. Gold moidores and more beside,
Jewels fit for a pirate's bride,
Down in that terrible hold we hide
With pieces of eight.

Chorus: With pieces of eight.

CHIEF. What do we care though we have to wade
Through rivers of blood ? 'Tis a roaring trade,
And the wages of fortune are freely paid
In pieces of eight.

Chorus: In pieces of eight.

Chorus: Every night between twelve and two,
There come the ghosts of the men we slew.
Every night from two to four
They guard the gold by the haunted shore,
Sparkling jewels and hefty plate
And pieces of eight. Pieces of eight.

(*At the end of it,* JILL *finds herself alone with* TUA-HEETA, *the Dusky Princess.*)

JILL (*fashionably*). I'm so pleased to meet my brother's future wife. It's so nice of you to come to see me. You will have some tea, won't you ? (*She puts out her hand and presses an imaginary bell.*) I wanted to see you, because I can tell you so many little things about my brother, which I think you ought to know. You see, Eric—my husband——

TUA-HEETA. Ereec ?

JILL. Yes. I wish you could see him. He's so nice-looking. But I'm afraid he won't be home to tea. That's the worst of marrying a sailor. They are away so much. Well, I was telling you about Oliver. I think it would be better if you knew at once that—he doesn't like rice-pudding.

TUA-HEETA. Rice-poodeeng ?

JILL. Yes, he hates it. It is very important that you should remember that. Then there's another thing—(*An untidy looking servant comes in. Can it be—can it possibly be* AUNT JANE ? *Horrors !*) He dislikes—— Oh, there you are, Jane. You've been a very long time answering the bell.

AUNT JANE. I'm so sorry ma'am, I was just dressing.

JILL. Excuses, Jane, always excuses. Leave me. Take a week's notice. (*To* TUA-HEETA.) You must excuse my maid. She's very stupid. Tea at once, Jane.

(AUNT JANE *sniffs and goes off.*)

What was I saying? Oh yes, about Oliver. He doesn't care for cod-liver oil in the way that some men do. You would be wise not to force it on him just at first. . . . Have you any idea where you are going to live?

TUA-HEETA. Live? (*These dusky maidens are no conversationists.*)

JILL. I expect Oliver will wish to reside at Hammersmith, so convenient for the City. You'll like Hammersmith. You'll go to St. Paul's Church, I expect. The Vicar will be sure to call.

(*Enter* AUNT JANE *with small tea-table.*)

Ah, here's tea. (*To* JANE.) You're very slow, Jane.

AUNT JANE. I'm sorry, ma'am.

JILL. It's no good being sorry. Take another week's notice. (*To* TUA-HEETA.) You must forgive my talking to my maid. She wants such a lot of looking after. (JANE *puts down the table.*) That will do, Jane. (JANE *bumps against the table.*) Dear, dear, how clumsy you are. What wages am I giving you now?

AUNT JANE. A shilling a month, ma'am.

JILL. Well, we'd better make it ninepence. (JANE *goes out in tears.*) Servants are a great nuisance, aren't they? Jane is a peculiarly stupid person. She used to be aunt to my brother, and I have only taken her on out of charity. (*She pours out from an imaginary teapot.*) Milk? Do you prefer it from the coco-nut or the cow? Sugar? (*She puts them in and hands the imaginary cup to* TUA-HEETA.)

TUA-HEETA. Thank you. (*Drinks.*)

JILL (*pouring herself a cup*). I hope you like China. (*She drinks, and then rings an imaginary bell.*) Well, as I was saying——

(*Enter* AUNT JANE.)

You can clear away, Jane.

AUNT JANE. Yes, ma'am.

(*She clears away the tea and* TUA-HEETA *and—very quickly—herself, as* OLIVER *comes back.* OLIVER *has been discussing boarding-tactics with his brother-in-law.* CAPTAIN CROOKSHANK *belongs to the now old-fashioned Marlinspike School;* OLIVER *is for well-primed pistols.*)

JILL. Oh, Oliver, I love your island. I've been thinking things all by myself. You're married to Tua-Heeta. You don't mind, do you?

OLIVER. Not at all, Jill. Make yourself at home. I've just been trying the doctor in the lagoon. There *were* sharks there, after all, so we'll have to find another place for bathing. Hullo, there's an elephant. What would you like to do now?

JILL. Just let's lie here and see what happens. (*What happens is that a cassowary comes along.*) Oh, what a lovely bird! Is it an ostrich?

(*The cassowary sniffs the air, puts its beak to the ground and goes off again.*)

OLIVER. Silly! It's a cassowary, of course.
JILL. What's a cassowary?
OLIVER. Jill! Don't you remember the rhyme?

> I wish I were a cassowary
> Upon the plains of Timbuctoo
> And then I'd eat a missionary—
> And hat and gloves and hymn book too!

JILL. Is that all they're for?
OLIVER. Well, what else would you want them for?

(*A* MISSIONARY, *pith-helmet, gloves, hymn-book, umbrella, all complete—creeps cautiously up. He bears a strong likeness to the curate, the* REVEREND SMILAX.)

MISSIONARY. I am sorry to intrude upon your privacy, dear friends, but have you observed a cassowary on this island, apparently looking for something?
OLIVER. Yes, we saw one just now.
MISSIONARY (*shuddering*). Dear, dear, dear. You didn't happen to ask him what was the object of his researches?
JILL. He went so quickly.
MISSIONARY (*coming out of the undergrowth to them*). I wonder if you have ever heard of a little rhyme which apparently attributes to the bird in question, when residing in the level pastures of Timbuctoo, an unholy lust for the body and appurtenances thereto of an unnamed clerical gentleman?
OLIVER
and   } (*shouting together*). Yes! Rather!
JILL
MISSIONARY. Dear, dear! Fortunately—I say fortunately—this is not Timbuctoo! (OLIVER *slips away and comes back with a notice-board " Timbuctoo," which he places at the edge of the trees, unseen by the* MISSIONARY, *who goes on talking to* JILL.) I take it that a cassowary residing in other latitudes is of a more temperate habit. His appetite, I venture to suggest, dear lady, would be under better restraint. That being so, I may perhaps safely—— (*He begins to move off, and comes suddenly up to the notice-board.*) Dear, dear, dear, dear, dear! This is terrible! You said, I think, that the—ah—bird in question was moving in *this* direction?
OLIVER. That's right.

MISSIONARY. Then I shall move, hastily, yet with all due precaution, in *that* direction. (*He walks off on tiptoe, looking over his shoulder in case the cassowary should reappear. Consequently, he does not observe the enormous* CANNIBAL *who has appeared from the trees on the right, until he bumps into him.*) I beg your—— (*He looks up.*) Dear, dear, dear, dear!
CANNIBAL. Boria, boria, boo!
MISSIONARY. Yes, my dear sir, it is as you say, a beautiful morning.
CANNIBAL. Boria, boria, boo!
MISSIONARY. But I was just going a little walk—in this direction—if you will permit me.
CANNIBAL (*threateningly*). Boria, boria, boo!
MISSIONARY. I have noticed it, my dear sir, I have often made that very observation to my parishioners.
CANNIBAL (*very threateningly*). Boria, boria, boo!
MISSIONARY. Oh, what's he saying?
OLIVER. He says it's his birthday to-morrow.
CANNIBAL. Wurra, wurra wug!
OLIVER. And will you come to the party?
MISSIONARY (*to* CANNIBAL). My dear sir, it is most kind of you to invite me, but a prior engagement in a different part of the country —a totally unexpected call upon me in another locality—will unfortunately——

(*While he is talking, the cassowary comes back, sidles up to him, and taps with his beak on the* MISSIONARY'S *pith-helmet.*)

MISSIONARY (*absently, without looking round*). Come in! . . . As I was saying, my dear sir—— (*The bird taps again. The* MISSIONARY *turns round annoyed.*) Can't you see I'm engaged—— Oh, dear, dear, dear, dear, dear!

HARD TIMES.

(*Trio :* CASSOWARY, MISSIONARY, *and* CANNIBAL.)

CASSOWARY. Hard times
For a poor young cassowary!
All life
Is nothing but a mass o' worry.
Hungry chicks who always cry,
Missionaries scarce and shy.

MISSIONARY. Hard times
For a hunted missionary.
No place
For an earnest visionary
I must leave this isle of fear,
Dear, dear, dear, dear, dear, dear.

CANNIBAL. Goo bah!
Gumshi kotshi-warry
Boo! Yah!
Tum-tum! Botshi-warry,
O-ah! O-ah! rumtifoo,
Boria, boria, boria, boo.

Chorus:

(*All sing their respective verses together, repeating the last two lines*).

(*Dance follows*).

(*The three of them go off together,* OLIVER *and* JILL *following eagerly behind to see who gets most.*)

(*The* PIRATES *come back, each carrying a small wooden ammunition-box.* PIRATES *music. They it round in a semicircle, the* PIRATE CHIEF *in the middle.*)

PIRATE. Steward! Steward!
STEWARD (*hurrying in*). Yes, sir, coming, sir.
CHIEF. Now then, tumble, up, my lad. I would carouse. Circulate the dry ginger.
STEWARD (*hurrying out*). Yes, sir, going, sir.
CHIEF. Look lively, my lad, look lively.
STEWARD (*hurrying in*). Yes, sir, coming, sir. (*He hands round mugs to them all.*)
CHIEF (*rising*). Gentlemen! (*They all stand up.*) The crew of the *Cocktail* will carouse—— (*They all take one step to the right, one back, and one left—which brings them behind their boxes—and then place their right feet on the boxes together.*) One! (*They raise their mugs.*) Two! (*They drink.*) Three! (*They bang down their mugs.*) Four! (*They wipe their mouths with the backs of their hands.*) So! . . . Steward!
STEWARD. Coming, sir.
CHIEF. The carouse is over.
STEWARD. Going, sir. (*He collects the mugs and goes out.*)

(*The* PIRATES *sit down again.*)

CHIEF (*addressing the men*). Having passed an hour thus in feasting and song——

(*Hark! is it the voice of our dear* MISS PINNIGER? *It is.*)

GOVERNESS (*off*). Oliver! Oliver! Jill! You may get up now and come down to tea.
CHIEF. Having, as I say, slept off our carouse——
GOVERNESS (*off*). Oliver! Jill! (*She comes in.*) Oh, I beg your pardon, I—er——

(*All the* PIRATES *rise and draw their weapons.*)

ACT II.] MAKE-BELIEVE. 39

CHIEF. Pray do not mention it. (*Polishing his pistol lovingly.*) You were asking——

GOVERNESS. I—I was l-looking for a small boy—Oliver——

CHIEF. Oliver? (*To* 1ST PIRATE.) Have we any Olivers on board?

1ST PIRATE. No, Captain. Only Bath Olivers.

CHIEF (*to* GOVERNESS). You cannot be referring to my brother-in-law, hight Two-Toed Thomas, the Terror of the Dyaks?

GOVERNESS. Oh no, no—— Just a small boy and his sister—Jill.

CHIEF (*to* 2ND PIRATE). Have we any Jills on board?

2ND PIRATE. No, Captain. Only gills of rum.

CHIEF (*to* GOVERNESS). You cannot be referring to Mrs. Crookshank, styled the Pride of the Pampas?

GOVERNESS. Oh, no, no, I am so sorry. Perhaps I—er——

CHIEF. Wait, woman. (*To* 6TH PIRATE.) Ernest, offer your seat to the lady.

(*The* 6TH PIRATE *stands up.*)

GOVERNESS (*nervously*). Oh please don't trouble, I'm getting out at the next station—I mean—I——

ALL PIRATES (*thunderously*). Sit down!

(*She sits down tremblingly and he stands by her with his pistol.*)

CHIEF. Thank you. (*To* 1ST PIRATE.) Cecil, have you your pencil and notebook with you?

1ST PIRATE (*producing them*). Ay, ay, Captain.

CHIEF. Then we will cross-examine the prisoner. (*To* GOVERNESS.) Name?

GOVERNESS. Pinniger.

1ST PIRATE (*writing*). Pincher.

CHIEF. Christian names, if any?

GOVERNESS. Letitia.

1ST PIRATE (*writing*). Letisher—how would you spell it, Captain?

CHIEF. Spell it like a sneeze. (*He sneezes.*) Age?

GOVERNESS. Twenty-three.

CHIEF (*to* 1ST PIRATE). Habits—untruthful. Appearance—against her. Got that?

1ST PIRATE. Yes, sir.

CHIEF (*to* GOVERNESS). And what are you for?

GOVERNESS. I teach. Oliver and Jill, you know.

CHIEF. And what do you teach them?

GOVERNESS. Oh, everything. Arithmetic, French, Geography, History, Dancing——

CHIEF (*holding up his hand*). A moment! I would take counsel with Percy. (*To* 2ND PIRATE.) Percy, what shall we ask her in Arithmetic? (*The* 2ND PIRATE *whispers to him.*) Excellent. (*To her.*) If you really are a teacher as you say, answer me this question.

The brigantine *Cocktail* is in longitude 40° 39' latitude 22° 50', sailing closehauled on the port tack at 8 knots in a 15-knot nor'-nor'-westerly breeze—how soon before she sights the Azores?

GOVERNESS. I—I—I'm afraid I—— You see—I——
CHIEF (*to* 1ST PIRATE). Arithmetic rotten.
1ST PIRATE (*writing*). Arithmetic rotten.
CHIEF (*to* 3RD PIRATE). Basil, ask her a question in French.
3RD PIRATE. What would the mate of a French frigate say if he wanted to say in French, "Avast there, ye lubbering swab" to a friend like?
GOVERNESS. Oh, but I hardly—I——
CHIEF (*to* 1ST PIRATE). French futile.
1ST PIRATE (*writing*). French futile.
CHIEF (*to* 4TH PIRATE). I don't suppose it's much use, Francis. But try her in Geography.
4TH PIRATE. Well now, lady. If you was wanting a nice creek to lay up cosy in, atween Dago Point and the Tortofitas, where would you run to?
GOVERNESS. R-run to? But that isn't—of course I——
CHIEF (*to* 1ST PIRATE). Geography ghastly.
1ST PIRATE (*writing*). Geography ghastly.
CHIEF (*to* 5TH PIRATE). Give her a last chance, Mervyn. See if she knows any history.
5TH PIRATE. I suppose you couldn't tell me what year it was when old John Cann took the *Saucy Codfish* over Black Tooth Reef and laid her alongside the Spaniard in the harbour there, and up comes the Don in his nightcap. "Shiver my timbers," he says in Spanish, "but there's only one man in the whole of the Spanish Main," he says, "and that's John Cann," he says, "who could——"

(*The* GOVERNESS *looks dumbly at him.*)

CHIEF. She couldn't. History hopeless.
1ST PIRATE. History hopeless.
CHIEF (*to* GOVERNESS). What else do you teach?
GOVERNESS. Music, dancing—er—but I don't think——
CHIEF. Steward!
STEWARD (*coming in*). Yes, sir, coming, sir.
CHIEF. Concertina.
STEWARD (*going out*). Yes, sir, going, sir.
CHIEF (*to* GOVERNESS). Can you dance a hornpipe?
GOVERNESS. No, I——
CHIEF. Dancing dubious.
STEWARD (*coming in*). Concertina, sir.
CHIEF Give it to the woman. (*He takes it to her.*)
GOVERNESS. I'm afraid I—— (*She produces one ghastly noise and drops the concertina in alarm.*)
1ST PIRATE (*writing*). What shall I say, sir? Music mouldy or music measly?

ACT II.] MAKE-BELIEVE.

CHIEF (*standing up*). Gentlemen, I think you will agree with me that the woman Pinniger has proved that she is utterly incapable of teaching anybody anything. (*The* PIRATES *growl.*) Twenty-five years, man and boy, I have sailed the Spanish Main, and with the possible exception of a dumb and half-witted nergo whom I shipped as cook in '64, I have never met anyone so profoundly lacking in intellect. I propose, therefore, that for the space of twenty-four hours the woman Pinniger should be incarcerated in the smuggler's cave, in the company of a black beetle of friendly temperament.

GOVERNESS. Mercy! Mercy!

1ST PIRATE. I should like to second that.

CHIEF. Those in favour—ay! (*They all say* "*Ay.*") Contrary —No! (*The* GOVERNESS *says* "*No.*") The motion is carried.

(*One of the* PIRATES *opens the door of the cave. The* GOVERNESS *rushes to the* CHIEF *and throws herself at his feet.* OLIVER *and* JILL *appear in the nick of time.*)

OLIVER. A maiden in distress! I will rescue her. (*She looks up and* OLIVER *recognizes her.*) Oh! Carry on, Commodore.

(*The* GOVERNESS *is lowered into the cave and the door is shut. Red glow in cave.*)

CHIEF (*to his men*). Go, find that black beetle, and having found it, introduce it circumspectly by the back door.

PIRATES. Ay, ay, sir.

(*They go out. Refrain of the* PIRATES, *music.*)

OLIVER. All the same, you know, I jolly well should like to rescue somebody.

JILL (*excitedly*). Oo, rescue me, Oliver.

CHIEF (*solemnly*). Two-toed Thomas, Terror of the Dyaks, and Pest of the North Pacific, truly thou art a well-plucked one. Wilt fight me for the wench? (*He puts an arm round* JILL.)

OLIVER. I will.

CHIEF. Swords?

OLIVER. Pistols.

CHIEF. At twenty paces?

OLIVER. Across a handkerchief.

CHIEF. Done! (*Feeling in his pockets.*) Have you got a handkerchief? I think I must have left mine on the dressing-table.

OLIVER (*bringing out his and putting it hastily back again*). Mine's rather—— Jill, haven't you got one?

JILL (*feeling*). I know I had one, but I——

CHIEF. This is an ill business. Five-and-thirty duels have I fought—and never before been delayed for lack of a handkerchief.

JILL. Ah, here it is. (*She produces a very small one and lays it on the ground. They stand each one side of it, pistols ready.*)

OLIVER. Jill, you must give the word.
JILL. Are you ready?

(*The sound of a gong is heard twice.*)

CHIEF. Listen! (*The gong is heard again.*) The Spanish Fleet is engaged!
JILL. *I* thought it was our tea gong.
CHIEF. Ah, perhaps you're right.
OLIVER. I say, we oughtn't to miss tea. (*Holding out his hand to her.*) Come on, Jill.
CHIEF. But you'll come back? We shall always be waiting here for you whenever you want us.
JILL. Yes, we'll come back, won't we, Oliver?
OLIVER. Oo, rather.

(*The whole population of the Island, Animals, PIRATES, and DUSKY MAIDENS, come on. They sing as they wave good-bye to the children, who are making their way to the boat.*)

JILL (*from the boat*). Good-bye, good-bye.
OLIVER. Good-bye, you chaps.
JILL (*politely*). And thank you all for a very pleasant afternoon.

GOOD-BYE, GOOD-BYE!

OLIVER *and* JILL. Good-bye to the island,
Good-bye, good-bye,
For the shadows of eve are falling,
And we hear far away
The clink of a tray,
And the voice of a tea gong calling.

PIRATES *and* DUSKY MAIDENS. Good-bye to the children,
Good-bye, good-bye,
But the waves of the seas of learning
Will wreck you once more
On this beautiful shore,
And our eyes shall behold you returning.

OMNES. Good-bye, good-bye, good-bye!

("Farewell" may be substituted for "Good-bye.")

(*They are all singing as the boat pushes off. Night comes on with tropical suddenness. The singing dies slowly down.*)

ACT III

FATHER CHRISTMAS AND THE HUBBARD FAMILY

SCENE I.—*The drawing-room of the* HUBBARDS *before Fame and Prosperity came to them. It is simply furnished with a deal table and two cane chairs.*

MR. *and* MRS. HUBBARD, *in faultless evening dress, are at home,* MR. HUBBARD *reading a magazine,* MRS. HUBBARD *with her hands in her lap. She sighs.*

MR. HUBBARD (*impetuously throwing down his magazine*). Dearest, you sighed?

MRS. HUBBARD (*quickly*). No, no, Henry. In a luxurious and well-appointed home such as this, why should I sigh?

MR. HUBBARD. True, dear. Not only is it artistically furnished, as you say, but it is also blessed with that most precious of all things —(*he lifts up the magazine*)—a library.

MRS. HUBBARD. Yes, yes, Henry, we have much to be thankful for.

MR. HUBBARD. We have indeed. But I am selfish. Would you care to read? (*He tears out a page of the magazine and hands it to her.*)

(*They both sit in silence for a little. She sighs again.*)

MR. HUBBARD. Darling, you did sigh. Tell me what grieves you.

MRS. HUBBARD. Little Isabel. Her cough troubles me.

MR. HUBBARD (*thoughtfully*). Isabel?

MRS. HUBBARD. Yes, dear, our youngest. Don't you remember, she comes after Harold?

MR. HUBBARD (*counting on his fingers*). A, B, C, D, E, F, G. H. I—dear me, have we got nine already?

MRS. HUBBARD (*imploringly*). Darling, say you don't think it's too many.

MR. HUBBARD. Oh no, no, not at all, my love. . . . After all, it isn't as if they were real children.

MRS. HUBBARD (*indignantly*). Henry! How can you say they are not real?

MR. HUBBARD. Well, I mean they're only the children we thought we'd like to have if Father Christmas gave us any.

MRS. HUBBARD. They are just as real to me as if they were here in the house. Ada, Bertram, Caroline, the high-spirited Dennis, pretty Elsie with the golden ringlets, dear little fair-haired Frank——

Mr. Hubbard (*firmly*). Darling one, Frank has curly brown hair. It was an understood thing that you should choose the girls, and *I* choose the boys. When we decided to take—A,B,C,D,E,F—a sixth child, it was my turn for a boy, and I selected Frank. He has curly brown hair and a fondness for animals.

Mrs. Hubbard. I daresay you're right, dear. Of course it is a little confusing when you never see your children.

Mr. Hubbard. Well, well, perhaps some day Father Christmas will give us some.

Mrs. Hubbard. Why does he neglect us so, Henry? We hang up our stockings every year, but he never seems to notice them. Even a diamond necklace or a few oranges or a five-shilling postal order would be something.

Mr. Hubbard. It is very strange. Possibly the fact that the chimney has not been swept for some years may have something to do with it. Or he may have forgotten our change of address. I cannot help feeling that if he knew how we had been left to starve in this way he would be very much annoyed.

Mrs. Hubbard. And clothes. I have literally nothing but what I am standing up in—I mean sitting down in.

Mr. Hubbard. Nor I, my love. But at least it will be written of us in the papers that the Hubbards perished in faultless evening dress. We are a proud race, and if Father Christmas deliberately cuts us off in this way, let us go down proudly. . . . Shall we go on reading or would you like to walk up and down the room? Fortunately these simple pleasures are left to us.

Mrs. Hubbard. I've finished this page.

Mr. Hubbard (*tearing out one*). Then let us walk, my love. (*They walk for a little while, until interrupted by a knock at the door.*)

Mrs. Hubbard. Some one at the door! Who could it be?

Mr. Hubbard (*getting up*). Just make the room look a little more homey, dear, in case it's anyone important.

(*He goes out leaving her to alter the position of the chairs slightly.*)

Mrs. Hubbard. Well?

Mr. Hubbard (*coming in*). A letter. (*He opens it.*)

Mrs. Hubbard. Quick!

Mr. Hubbard (*whistling with surprise*). Father Christmas! An invitation to Court! (*Reading.*) "Father Christmas at Home, 25th December. Jollifications, 11.59 p.m." My love, he has found us at last! (*They embrace each other.*)

Mrs. Hubbard. Henry, how gratifying!

Mr. Hubbard. Yes. (*Sadly, after a pause.*) But we can't go.

Mrs. Hubbard (*sadly*). No, I have no clothes.

Mr. Hubbard. Nor I.

Mrs. Hubbard. How can I possibly go without a diamond

necklace? None of the Montmorency-Smythe women has ever been to Court without a diamond necklace.

Mr. Hubbard. The Hubbards are a proud race. No male Hubbard would dream of appearing at Court without a gentleman's gold Albert watch-chain. . . . Besides, there is another thing. There will be many footmen at Father Christmas's Court, who will doubtless require coppers pressed into their palms. My honour would be seriously affected, were I compelled to whisper to them that I had no coppers.

Mrs. Hubbard. It is very unfortunate. Father Christmas may have hundreds of presents waiting for us.

Mr. Hubbard. True. But how would it be to hang up our stockings again this evening—now that we know he knows we are here? I would suggest tied on to the door-knocker, to save him the trouble of coming down the chimney.

Mrs. Hubbard (*excitedly*). Henry, I wonder! But of course we will.

(*They begin to take off—the one a sock, the other a stocking.*)

Mr. Hubbard. I almost wish now that my last suit had been a knickerbocker one. However, we must do what we can with a sock.

Mrs. Hubbard (*holding up her stocking and looking at it a little anxiously*). I hope Father Christmas won't give me a bicycle. A stocking never sets so well after it has had a bicycle in it.

Mr. Hubbard (*taking it from her*). Now, dear, I will go down and put them in position. Let us hope that fortune will be kind to us.

Mrs. Hubbard. Let us hope so, darling. And quickly. For (*picking up her page of the magazine*) it is a trifle cold.

(*He goes out and she is left reading.*)

(*Black out follows.*)

Scene II.—*Outside the house the snow lies deep. The stocking and sock are tied on to the door-knocker. There is a light in the window.*

A party of carol-singers, with lanterns, come by and halt in the snow outside the house.

Peter Ableways. Friends, are we all assembled?

Jonas Humphrey. Ay, ay, Peter Ableways, assembled and met together in a congregation, for the purpose of lifting up our voices in joyous thanksgiving, videlicet the singing of a carol or other wintry melody.

Martha Porritt. Are we to begin soon, Master Ableways? My feet are cold.

Jennifer. Ay, let's begin, Peter Ableways, while we carry the tune in our heads.

Peter. Are we all ready, friends? I will say one—two—

—three—and at "three" I pray you all to give it off in a hearty manner from the chest. One—two——

JONAS. Hold, hold, Master Ableways! Does it begin—— No, that's the other one. (JENNIFER *whispers the first line to him*.) Ay, ay—I have it now—and bursting to get out of me. Proceed, Peter Ableways.

PETER. One—two—three—— (*They carol*.)

CAROL.

The holly and the ivy tree,
They grow so fair and green,
With laurel and with mistletoe
Most pleasant to be seen.
And we are come to you this night,
To wish you all good cheer,
A merry Christmas, gentlemen,
And a right glad New Year.

Refrain : Wassail! Wassail!
All men on earth be glad this day.
Wassail! Wassail!
Rejoice my masters while ye may,
And send ye all have grateful hearts
According to your store,
And ne'er forget the singers here
That carol at your door.

The wine is red within the cup,
And dark and brown the ale,
And while good liquor floweth free
The heart shall never fail,
Then of your plenty, gentlemen,
We pray you something spare,
For it shall make ye all thrice blest
Your blessings for to share.

Refrain : Wassail! Wassail! etc.

PETER. Well sung, all.

MARTHA. Don't forget the collection, Master Ableways.

PETER. Ay, the collection. (*He takes off his hat and places it on the ground*.)

HUMPHREY. Nay, not so fast, Master Peter. Where money is, money will come.

JENNIFER. Ay, it makes a pleasing clink.

PETER. True, Mistress Jennifer. Master Humphrey speaks true. (*He pours some coppers from his pockets into his hat*.)

MARTHA. Are we to go on, Master Ableways? My feet are cold.

PETER (*shaking the hat*). So, a warming noise.

HUMPHREY. To it, again, gentles.

PETER. Are all ready? One—two—three! (*They carol*.)

PETER. Well sung, all.

HUMPHREY. Have you the hat, Master Peter?

ACT III.]   MAKE-BELIEVE.   47

PETER (*picking it up*). Ay, friend, all is ready.
(*The door opens and* MR. HUBBARD *appears at the entrance.*)
MR. HUBBARD. Good evening, friends.
PETER. Good evening, sir. (*He holds out the hat.*)
MR. HUBBARD (*looking at it*). What is this? (PETER *shakes it.*) Aha! Money!
PETER. Remember the carol singers, sir.
MR. HUBBARD (*helping himself*). My dear friends, I will always remember you. This is most generous. I shall never forget your kindness. This is most unexpected. But not the less welcome, not the less—— I think there's a ha'penny down there that I missed—thank you. As I was saying, unexpected but welcome. I thank you heartily. Good evening, friends.

(*He goes in and shuts the door.*)

PETER (*who has been too surprised to do anything but keep his mouth open*). Well! ... Well! ... Well, friends, let us to the next house. We have got all that we can get here.

(*They trail off silently.*)

MARTHA (*as they go off*). Master Ableways!
PETER. Ay, lass!
MARTHA. My feet aren't so cold now.

(*But this is to be an exciting night. As soon as they are gone, a Burglar and a Burglaress steal into view.*)

BILL. Wotcher get, Liz? (*She holds up a gold watch and chain. He nods and holds up a diamond necklace.*) 'Ow's that?
LIZ (*starting suddenly*). H'st!
BILL (*in a whisper*). What is it?
LIZ. Copper!
BILL (*desperately*). 'Ere, quick, get rid of these. 'Ide 'em in the snow, or——
LIZ. Bill! (*He turns round.*) Look! (*She points to the stocking and sock hanging up.*) We can come back for 'em as soon as 'e's gone.

(BILL *looks at them, and back at her, and grins. He drops the necklace into one and the watch into the other. As the* POLICEMAN *approaches they strike up, " While shepherds watched their flock by night," with an air of enthusiasm.*)

POLICEMAN. Now then, move along there.

(*They move along. The* POLICEMAN *flashes his light on the door to see that all is well. The stocking and sock are revealed. He beams sentimentally at them and goes off.* HUBBARD *opens door, takes down stocking and sock and goes in.*)

SCENE III.—*We are inside the house again.* MRS. HUBBARD *is still reading a page of the magazine. In dashes* MR. HUBBARD *with the sock and stocking.*

MR. HUBBARD. My darling, what do you think? Father Christmas has sent you a little present. (*He hands her the stocking.*)

MRS. HUBBARD. Henry! Has he sent you one too?

MR. HUBBARD (*holding up his sock*). Observe!

MRS. HUBBARD. How sweet of him! I wonder what mine is. What is yours, darling?

MR. HUBBARD. I haven't looked yet, my love. Perhaps just a few nuts or something of that sort, with a card attached saying, "To wish you the old, old wish." We must try not to be disappointed, whatever it is, darling.

MRS. HUBBARD. Of course, Henry. After all, it is the kindly thought which really matters.

MR. HUBBARD. Certainly. All the same, I hope—— Will you look in yours, dear, first, or shall I?

MRS. HUBBARD. I think I should like to, darling. (*Feeling it.*) It feels so exciting. (*She brings out a diamond necklace.*) Henry!

MR. HUBBARD. My love! (*They embrace.*) Now you will be able to go to Court. You must say that your husband is unfortunately in bed with a bad cold. You can tell me all about it when you come home. I shall be able to amuse myself with—— (*He is feeling in his sock while talking, and now brings out the watch and chain.*)

MRS. HUBBARD. Henry! My love!

MR. HUBBARD. A gentleman's gold hunter and Albert watch-chain. My darling!

(*They put down their presents on the table and embrace each other again.*)

MRS. HUBBARD. Let's put them on at once, Henry, and see how they suit us.

MR. HUBBARD. Allow me, my love. (*He fastens her necklace.*)

MRS. HUBBARD (*happily*). Now I feel really dressed again! Oh, I wish we had a looking-glass.

MR. HUBBARD (*opening his gold watch*). Try in here, my darling.

MRS. HUBBARD (*surveying herself*). How perfectly sweet! . . . Now let me put your watch-chain on for you, dear. (*She arranges it for him—*HENRY *very proud.*)

MR. HUBBARD. Does it suit me, darling?

MRS. HUBBARD. You look fascinating, Henry!

(*They strut about the room with an air.*)

MR. HUBBARD (*taking out his watch and looking at it ostentatiously*). Well, well, we ought to be starting. My watch makes it 11.58. (*He holds it to her ear.*) Hasn't it got a sweet tick?

MRS. HUBBARD. Sweet! But starting where, Henry? Do you mean we can really—— But you haven't any money.

MR. HUBBARD. Money? (*Taking out a handful.*) Heaps of it.

ACT III.]   MAKE-BELIEVE.   49

Mrs. Hubbard. Father Christmas?
Mr. Hubbard. Undoubtedly, my love. Brought round to the front door just now by some of his messengers. By the way, dear— (*indicating the sock and stocking*)—hadn't we better put these on before we start?
Mrs. Hubbard. Of course. How silly of me!
(*They sit down and put them on.*)
Mr. Hubbard. Really, this is a very handsome watch-chain.
Mrs. Hubbard. It becomes you admirably, Henry.
Mr. Hubbard. Thank you, dear. There's just one little point. Father Christmas is sometimes rather shy about acknowledging the presents he gives. He hates being thanked. If, therefore, he makes any comment on your magnificent necklace or my handsome watch-chain, we must say that they have been in the family for some years.
Mrs. Hubbard. Of course, dear. (*They get up.*)
Mr. Hubbard. Well, now we're ready.
Mrs. Hubbard. Darling one, don't you think we might bring the children?
Mr. Hubbard. Of course, dear! How forgetful of me!... Children—'shun! (*Listen! Their heels click as they come to attention.*) Number! (*Their voices—alternate boy and girl, one to nine —are heard.*) Right *turn!*
Mrs. Hubbard. Darling one, I almost seem to hear them!
Mr. Hubbard. Are you ready, my love?
Mrs. Hubbard. Yes, Henry.
Mr. Hubbard. Quick march!

(*The children are heard tramping off. Very proudly* Mr. *and* Mrs. Hubbard *bring up the rear.*)

Scene IV.—*The Court of* Father Christmas. *Shall we describe it? No. But there is everything which any reasonable person could want, from ices to catapults. And the decorations, done in candy so that you can break off a piece whenever you are hungry, are superb.*

1st Usher (*from the back*). Father Christmas!
Several Ushers (*from the front*). Father Christmas! (*He comes in.*)
Father Christmas (*genially*). Good evening, everybody.

(*I ought to have said that there are already some hundreds of people there, though how some of them got invitations—but, after all, that is not our business. Wishing to put them quite at their ease,* Father Christmas, *who has a very creditable baritone, gives them a song.*)

KING OF THE LAND OF YULE.

(*Song:* Father Christmas.)

I'm absolute King of the Land of Yule,
And nobody dares to dispute my rule,
For my methods are drastic, short and quick,

D

At the very first hint of a Bolshevik.
In every land I keep my state
And I never intend to abdicate.

Chorus : Crown him with laurel and holly,
Hang up the mistletoe bough,
Never was monarch more jolly
Than he who reigns over us now.
Ring out the bells from each steeple,
Cheer him who brings us good cheer,
Welcome him, all little people,
Old Father Christmas is here.

A bold bad boy there perchance may be
Who says that he doesn't believe in me,
Who dares the laws of my realm to slight,
And whose stocking is not hung up at night,
But his punishment comes when he sees the toys.
That I give to my faithful girls and boys.

Chorus : Crown him with laurel and holly, etc.

But I never despise a mortal's aid,
For addresses will sometimes get mislaid.
If you know of a child who is sad and poor,
And I happen to miss that humble door,
Why you know I will bless that generous heart
That understudies my kingly part.

Chorus : Crown him with laurel and holly, etc.

(*After the applause which follows it, he retires to the throne at the back, and awaits his more important guests. The* USHERS *take up their places, one at the entrance, one close to the throne.*)

1ST USHER. Mr. and Mrs. Henry Hubbard! (*They come in.*)

MR. HUBBARD (*pressing twopence into his palm*). Thank you, my man, thank you.

2ND USHER. Mr. and Mrs. Henry Hubbard.

MR. HUBBARD (*handing out another twopence*). Not at all, my man, not at all.

(MRS. HUBBARD *curtsies and* MR. HUBBARD *bows to* FATHER CHRISTMAS.)

FATHER CHRISTMAS. I am delighted to welcome you to my Court. How are you both?

MR. HUBBARD. Very well, thank you, sir. My wife has a slight cold in one foot, owing to——

MRS. HUBBARD (*hastily*). A touch of gout, sir, inherited from my ancestors, the Montmorency-Smythes.

FATHER CHRISTMAS. Dear me, it won't prevent you dancing, I hope?

MRS. HUBBARD. Oh no, sir.

FATHER CHRISTMAS. That's right. We shall have a few more friends coming in soon. You have been giving each other presents already, I see. I congratulate you, madam, on your husband's taste.

MRS. HUBBARD (*touching her necklace*). Oh no, this is a very old heirloom of the Montmorency-Smythe family.

MR. HUBBARD. An ancestress of Mrs. Hubbard's—a lady-in-waiting at the Tottenham Court—at the Tudor Court—was fortunate enough to catch the eye of—er——

MRS. HUBBARD. Elizabeth.

MR. HUBBARD. Queen Elizabeth, and—er——

FATHER CHRISTMAS. I see. You are lucky, madam, to have such beautiful jewels. (*Turning to* MR. HUBBARD.) And this delightful gold Albert watch-chain——

MR. HUBBARD. Presented to an ancestor of mine, Sir Humphrey de Hubbard, at the battle of—er——

MRS. HUBBARD. Agincourt.

MR. HUBBARD. As you say, dear, Agincourt. By King Richard the—I should say William the—well, by the King.

FATHER CHRISTMAS. How very interesting.

MR. HUBBARD. Yes. My ancestor clove a scurvy knave from the chaps to the chine. I don't quite know how you do that, but I gather that he inflicted some sort of a scratch upon his adversary, and the King rewarded him with this handsome watch-chain.

USHERS (*announcing*). Mr. Robinson Crusoe! (*He comes in.*)

FATHER CHRISTMAS. How do you do?

CRUSOE (*bowing*). I'm a little late, I'm afraid, sir. My raft was delayed by adverse gales.

(FATHER CHRISTMAS *introduces him to the* HUBBARDS, *who inform him that the weather is very seasonable.*)

USHERS. Miss Riding Hood! (*She comes in.*)

FATHER CHRISTMAS. How do you do?

RIDING HOOD (*curtseying*). I hope I am in time, sir. I had to look in on my grandmother on the way here.

(FATHER CHRISTMAS *makes the necessary introductions.*)

MRS. HUBBARD (*to* CRUSOE). Do come and see me, Mr. Crusoe. Any Friday. I should like your advice about my parrot. He's moulting in all the wrong places.

MR. HUBBARD (*to* RED RIDING HOOD). I don't know if you're interested in wolves at all, Miss Hood. I heard a very good story about one the other day. (*He begins to tell it, but she has hurried away before he can remember whether it was Thursday or Friday.*)

USHERS. Baron Bluebeard! (*He comes in.*)

FATHER CHRISTMAS. How do you do?

BLUEBEARD (*bowing*). I trust you have not been waiting for me, sir. I had a slight argument with my wife before starting, which delayed me somewhat.

(FATHER CHRISTMAS *forgives him.*)

USHERS. Princess Goldilocks!
FATHER CHRISTMAS. How do you do?
GOLDILOCKS (*curtseying*). I brought the youngest bear with me—do you mind? (*She introduces the youngest bear to* FATHER CHRISTMAS *and the other guests.*) Say, how do you do, darling? (*To an* USHER.) Will you give him a little porridge, please, and if you have got a nice bed where he could rest a little afterwards—he gets tired so quickly.
USHER. Certainly, your Royal Highness.
GOLDILOCKS (*to* CRUSOE). Come along and dance with me.
CRUSOE. I am a little out of practice—er—but if you don't mind —er—— (*He comes.*)

(*The music of* GOLDILOCKS' *dance begins.*)

BLUEBEARD (*to* RIDING HOOD). May I have the pleasure?
MRS. HUBBARD (*to* RIDING HOOD). Be careful, dear; he has a very bad reputation.
RIDING HOOD (*to* BLUEBEARD). You don't eat people, do you?
BLUEBEARD (*pained by this injustice*). Never!
RIDING HOOD. Oh then, I don't mind. But I do hate being eaten.

(*Now we can't possibly describe the whole dance to you, for in every corner of the big ballroom couples were revolving and sliding, and making small talk with each other. So we will just take two specimen conversations.*)

CRUSOE (*nervous, poor man*). Princess Goldilocks, may I speak to you on a matter of some importance to me?
GOLDILOCKS. I wish you would.
CRUSOE (*looking across at* BLUEBEARD *and* RED RIDING HOOD, *who are revolving close by*). Alone.
GOLDILOCKS (*to* BLUEBEARD). Do you mind? You can have your turn afterwards.
BLUEBEARD (*to* RIDING HOOD). Shall we adjourn to the Buffet?
RIDING HOOD. Oh, do let's.

(*They adjourn.*)

CRUSOE (*bravely*). Princess, I am a lonely man.
GOLDILOCKS (*encouragingly*). Yes, Robinson?
CRUSOE. I am not much of a one for society, and I don't quite know how to put these things, but—er—if you would like to share my island, I—I should so love to have you there.
GOLDILOCKS. Oh, Bobbie!
CRUSOE (*warming to it*). I have a very comfortable house, and a man-servant, and an excellent view from the south windows, and several thousands of acres of good rough-shooting, and—oh, do say you'll come!
GOLDILOCKS. May I bring my bears with me?

CRUSOE. Of course! I ought to have said that. I have a great fondness for animals.

(*They go out. Now it is the other couple's turn.*)

(*Enter, then,* BLUEBEARD *and* RIDING HOOD)

BLUEBEARD. Perhaps I ought to tell you at once, Miss Riding Hood, that I have been married before.
RIDING HOOD. Yes?
BLUEBEARD. My last wife unfortunately died just before I started out here this evening.
RIDING HOOD (*calmly*). Did you kill her?
BLUEBEARD (*taken aback*). I—I—I——
RIDING HOOD. Are you quite a nice man, Bluebeard?
BLUEBEARD. W-what do you mean? I am a very *rich* man. If you will marry me, you will live in a wonderful castle, full of everything you want.
RIDING HOOD. That will be rather jolly.
BLUEBEARD (*dramatically*). But there is one room into which you must never go. (*Holding up a key.*) Here is the key of it. (*He offers it to her.*)
RIDING HOOD (*indifferently*). But if I'm never to go into it, I shan't want the key.
BLUEBEARD (*upset*). You—you *must* have the key.
RIDING HOOD. Why?
BLUEBEARD. The—the others all had it.
RIDING HOOD (*coldly*). Bluebeard, you aren't going to talk about your *other* wives all the time, are you?
BLUEBEARD. N—no.
RIDING HOOD. Then don't be silly. And take this key, and go and tidy up that ridiculous room of yours, and when it's nice and clean, and when you've shaved off that absurd beard, perhaps I'll marry you.
BLUEBEARD (*furiously drawing his sword*). Madam!
RIDING HOOD. Don't do it here. You'll want some hot water.
BLUEBEARD (*trying to put his sword back*). This is too much, this is——
RIDING HOOD. You're putting it in the wrong way round.
BLUEBEARD (*stiffly*). Thank you. (*He manages to get it in.*)
RIDING HOOD. Well, do you want to marry me?
BLUEBEARD. Yes!
RIDING HOOD. Sure?
BLUEBEARD (*admiringly*). More than ever. You're the first woman I've met who hasn't been afraid of me.
RIDING HOOD (*surprised*). Are you very alarming? Wolves frighten me sometimes, but not just silly men. . . . (*Giving him her hand.*) All right then. But you'll do what I said?
BLUEBEARD. Beloved one, I will do anything for you.

(CRUSOE *and* GOLDILOCKS *come back. Probably it will occur to the four of them to sing a song indicative of the happy family life awaiting them. On the other hand they may prefer to dance. . . .*)

(*But enough of this. Let us get on to the great event of the evening. Ladies and gentlemen, are you all assembled ? Then silence, please, for* FATHER CHRISTMAS.)

FATHER CHRISTMAS. Ladies and gentlemen, it gives me great pleasure to see you here at my Court this evening; and in particular my friends Mr. and Mrs. Hubbard, of whom I have been too long neglectful. However, I hope to make up for it to-night. (*To an* USHER.) Disclose the Christmas Tree!

(*The Christmas Tree is disclosed, and—what do you think? Children disguised as crackers are hanging from every branch! Well, I never!*)

FATHER CHRISTMAS (*quite calmly*). Distribute the presents!

(*An* USHER *takes down the children one by one and places them in a row, reading from the labels on them,* "MRS. HUBBARD, MR. HUBBARD" *alternately.*)

USHER (*handing list to* MR. HUBBARD). Here is the nominal roll, sir.

MR. HUBBARD (*looking at it in amazement*). What's this? (MRS. HUBBARD *looks over his shoulder*) Ada, Bertram, Caroline—My darling one!

MRS. HUBBARD. Henry! Our children at last! Oh, are they all—*all* there?

MR. HUBBARD. We'll soon see, dear. Ada!

ADA (*springing to attention*). Father! (*She stands at ease.*)

MR. HUBBARD. Bertram! . . . (*And so on up to* ELSIE.) . . . Frank!

FRANK. Father!

MR. HUBBARD. There you are, darling, I told you he had curly hair. . . . Gwendoline! (*And so on.*)

MRS. HUBBARD (*to* FATHER CHRISTMAS). Oh thank you so much. It is sweet of you.

MR. HUBBARD (*to* FATHER CHRISTMAS). We are slightly overcome. Do you mind if we just dance it off. (FATHER CHRISTMAS *nods genially.*) Come on, children!

(*He holds out his hands, and he and his wife and the children dance round in a ring singing,* "Here we go round the Christmas Tree, all on a Christmas evening." . . .)

And then—— But at this moment JAMES and ROSEMARY and the HUBBARD *children stopped thinking, so of course the play came to an end. And if there were one or two bits in it which the children didn't quite understand, that was* JAMES'S *fault. He never ought to have been thinking at all, really.*

www.ingramcontent.com/pod-product-compliance
Ingram Content Group UK Ltd.
Pitfield, Milton Keynes, MK11 3LW, UK
UKHW021848210426
53221PUK00022B/534